UNITED NATIONS CONFERENCE ON TRADE AND DEVELOPMENT

Technical and statistical report

Fast-tracking implementation of reforms enabling e-commerce and digital trade

2025

United Nations
Geneva, 2025

United Nations Publications
405 East 42nd Street
New York, New York 10017
United States of America
Email: publications@un.org
Website: https://shop.un.org

This publication has been edited externally.

United Nations publication issued by the United Nations
Conference on Trade and Development

UNCTAD/DTL/ECDE/2025/4
ISBN: 978-92-1-154506-7
eISBN: 978-92-1-158864-4
Sales No. E.25.II.D.35

Acknowledgements

The present report was prepared by Alessandro Vitale and Iris Macculi, under the overall guidance of Martine Julsaint Kidane and Cécile Barayre, of the Division on Technology and Logistics of the United Nations Conference on Trade and Development (UNCTAD). It is the fourth report of a series conducted by the E-commerce and Digital Economy Branch of UNCTAD, through the eTrade Implementation Support Mechanism.

UNCTAD gratefully acknowledges the valuable efforts of the network of eTrade focal points in mobilizing stakeholders and collecting data for the present report. From Africa: Kouakou Charles Yao (Ministry of Commerce and Industry, Côte d'Ivoire), Michael Wairoma (State Department for Trade, Kenya), Fatsani Ngalande (Ministry of Trade and Industry, Malawi), Matchiane Bacar (Ministry of Digital Transformation, Innovation and Modernization of Administration, Mauritania), Ibrahim Tanda Bonkano (Ministry of Trade and Private Sector Promotion, the Niger), Jean Premier Bienvenu Rukundo (Ministry of Trade and Industry, Rwanda), Fara Makha Diop (Ministry of Industry and Trade, Senegal), Rachid Darago (Ministry of Trade, Handicrafts and Local Consumption, Togo), Khabbab Hadhri (Ministry of Trade and Export Development, Tunisia), Chris Matsiko (Ministry of Trade, Industry and Cooperatives, Uganda), David Geofrey (Ministry of Industry and Trade, United Republic of Tanzania) and Eric Sichembe (Ministry of Commerce, Trade and Industry, Zambia). From Asia: Md. Sayed Ali (Ministry of Commerce, Bangladesh), Chea Laichea (Ministry of Commerce, Cambodia), Fatema Shneekat (Ministry of Industry, Trade and Supply, Jordan), Enkhbold Vorshilov (Ministry of Foreign Affairs, Mongolia) and Lila Dhar Adhikari (Ministry of Industry, Commerce and Supplies, Nepal). From Latin America and the Caribbean: Darwin Herber Carrasco Rosas (Secretariat of Government and Digital Transformation, Peru). From the Pacific: Karen Niumata (Ministry of Commerce, Industry and Labour, Samoa), Richard Nokia (Ministry of Commerce, Industry, Labour and Immigration, Solomon Islands), Kathleen Walters (Ministry of Trade and Economic Development, Tonga), Falaoa Sione (Ministry of Foreign Affairs, Labour and Trade, Tuvalu) and Francisca Miller (Ministry of Trade and Commerce, Vanuatu).

The support of the Permanent Missions in Geneva of the countries under review was instrumental in coordinating and eliciting contributions from their respective capitals. Their engagement was instrumental in ensuring the comprehensiveness of the report. UNCTAD also gratefully acknowledges the representatives of regional organizations who participated in the review: Angelique Umulisa (East African Community secretariat), Kolawole Sofola (Commission of the Economic Community of West African States) and Andrea Ibba (Pacific Islands Forum secretariat).

The report also benefited from the inputs of eTrade for all partners, in particular the International Civil Aviation Organization, the United Nations Commission on International Trade Law and the Universal Postal Union.

This publication was edited by Robert Blackwell. Desktop publishing and cover design were provided by Keel Chan. Administrative support was provided by Diana Quiros.

UNCTAD expresses particular appreciation to the core donors to the UNCTAD E-commerce and Digital Economy Programme, namely Australia, Germany, the Kingdom of the Netherlands, Sweden and Switzerland, for their financial support.

Foreword

In an era in which digital transformation is fast reshaping the global economy, having the ability to harness the potential of e-commerce and digital trade is essential for developing countries.

The fourth eTrade Implementation Review provides a timely and comprehensive analysis of how partner countries and regions are translating digital ambitions into specific action. Covering 23 countries and three regional organizations, the review reflects a rich mosaic of experiences, capturing both progress made and remaining challenges.

The review underscores the value of our eTrade Implementation Support Mechanism in supporting countries to move beyond diagnostics and into implementation, while fostering national ownership, inclusive dialogue and regional cooperation. In the review, valuable lessons drawn from various contexts offer a practical resource for policymakers, development partners and stakeholders committed to inclusive digital growth.

Meaningful progress is more likely when e-commerce and digital trade are prioritized at the national level, efforts are well coordinated and policies are supported through inclusive, multistakeholder collaboration. Many of those efforts are taking place under challenging circumstances, amid cascading global crises, persistent inequalities, fast-moving technological shifts and a decline in official development assistance. Yet, the pace of change needs to accelerate. Institutional and operational capacities remain uneven. Persistent gaps in information and communications technology connectivity and trade logistics, regulatory frameworks, digital payment systems, digital skills, access to financing and trust continue to hold back the full potential of e-commerce and digital trade. Strengthening evidence-based policymaking, interministerial coordination, multistakeholder dialogue and sustained capacity-building efforts will be key to unlocking broader development impacts.

In that context, the Global Digital Compact has further stressed the importance of aligning efforts towards a more inclusive and sustainable digital future. UNCTAD, through its convening power, technical expertise and partnerships, notably through the eTrade for all initiative, plays a pivotal role in supporting countries to navigate that evolving landscape. By connecting the dots between national priorities, regional strategies and global commitments, we will continue to help ensure that digitalization works for development and for all.

Torbjörn Fredriksson
Head, E-commerce and Digital Economy Branch
Division on Technology and Logistics

Table of contents

Figures

Tables

Boxes

Abbreviations

AfCFTA	African Continental Free Trade Area
AI	artificial intelligence
ASEAN	Association of Southeast Asian Nations
ASYCUDA	Automated System for Customs Data
EAC	East African Community
ECOWAS	Economic Community of West African States
EIF	Enhanced Integrated Framework
eT	eTrade
GIZ	German Agency for International Cooperation
ICT	information and communications technology
ITC	International Trade Centre
ITU	International Telecommunication Union
MSMEs	micro-, small and medium-sized enterprises
OECD	Organisation for Economic Co-operation and Development
PIF	Pacific Islands Forum
PAPSS	Pan-African Payment and Settlement System
RTGS	real-time gross settlement
SMEs	small and medium-sized enterprises
UN	United Nations Capital Development Fund
UNCITRAL	United Nations Commission on International Trade Law
UNCTAD	United Nations Conference on Trade and Development
UNDP	United Nations Development Programme
UPU	Universal Postal Union
WAEMU	West African Economic and Monetary Union
WTO	World Trade Organization

Note

Within the Division on Technology and Logistics of UNCTAD, the E-commerce and Digital Economy Branch carries out policy-oriented analytical work on the development implications of information and communications technology (ICT), e-commerce and the digital economy. It is responsible for the preparation of the Digital Economy Report, as well as thematic studies on ICT for development.

The Branch promotes international dialogue on issues related to ICT for development and contributes to building the capacities of developing countries to measure the digital economy and to design and implement relevant policies and legal frameworks. It also monitors the global status of e-commerce legislation (the Global Cyberlaw Tracker). Since 2016, the Branch has coordinated a multi-stakeholder initiative, eTrade for all, which is aimed at improving the ability of developing countries, particularly least developed countries, to use and benefit from e-commerce. The initiative is also behind the UNCTAD eTrade for Women initiative, launched in 2019, which is aimed at promoting a more inclusive digital economy, in particular, through its network of Advocates. Those women digital entrepreneurs are active in all developing regions and contribute to capacity-building, mentoring and awareness-raising activities for more inclusive gender policies.

Reference to companies and their activities should not be construed as an endorsement by UNCTAD of those companies or their activities. References to "$" means United States of America dollars.

Executive summary

Bridging the digital readiness gap is not simply a development challenge, it is a prerequisite for inclusive and equitable participation in the global economy. As digitalization accelerates and reshapes trade, production and consumption patterns, countries that lack foundational digital infrastructure, enabling policies and institutional capabilities risk falling further behind. Many developing countries, especially least developed countries, remain on the margins of the digital economy, and micro-, small and medium-sized enterprises (MSMEs) continue to face major barriers to access and effective participation.

While a growing number of developing countries have now adopted e-commerce strategies or policies, based on informed diagnostics, translating these strategies into action remains a challenge. In the present report, which is the fourth eTrade Implementation Review, the urgency of accelerating reforms that enable digital trade is highlighted, particularly in areas such as information and communications technology (ICT) infrastructure, legal and regulatory frameworks, data governance, payments and skills development. Encouragingly, some countries have made notable progress, including through investments in broadband infrastructure, legal modernization and the expansion of digital financial services. However, the overall pace and scale of reform remain uneven, calling for greater attention to critical enablers, such as reliable and widespread electricity, basic literacy and access to content in local languages.

Integrating e-commerce more centrally into national development and trade agendas is essential to unlock its full potential for innovation, job and value creation and economic resilience. Strengthening implementation efforts, supported by coordinated technical assistance and development partner collaboration, will be critical to ensure that digital transformation contributes meaningfully to sustainable and inclusive growth.

The fourth review is built upon previous reports[1] and incorporates a more refined and responsive approach, shaped by continuous feedback from partner countries. It is focused on the progress reported by 23 countries:

- Africa: Côte d'Ivoire, Kenya, Malawi, Mauritania, Niger, Rwanda, Senegal, Togo, Tunisia, Uganda, United Republic of Tanzania and Zambia
- Asia: Bangladesh, Cambodia, Jordan, Mongolia and Nepal
- Latin America and the Caribbean: Peru
- Pacific: Samoa, Solomon Islands, Tonga, Tuvalu and Vanuatu

It contains dedicated country case studies of Cambodia, Kenya and Vanuatu (annex I). Moreover, ad hoc references are made to other countries' experiences based on desk research, all with a view to providing a broad picture of global progress and the remaining challenges. The research methodology is presented in annex II.

The review comprises two main parts:

- A review of national and regional e-commerce development policy frameworks, governance and monitoring mechanisms, data availability for evidence-based and participatory policymaking, as well as the role of capacity-building to strengthen e-commerce policymaking.
- Specific evidence of progress and achievements of countries and regions in their

[1] UNCTAD (2020, 2022a and 2023b).

implementation of eTrade Readiness Assessment (eT Ready) recommendations, and e-commerce policies and strategies, as well as persistent challenges. It showcases broader e-commerce ecosystem developments and impactful national and regional initiatives for businesses and consumers in various areas.

A. Improving policymaking to foster a thriving e-commerce environment

As at July 2025, 38 countries and two regional organizations had benefited from the eT Readies of the United Nations Conference on Trade and Development (UNCTAD) (figure I), which provide a comprehensive diagnostic of policy gaps and opportunities across essential policy areas. Those assessments often serve as catalysts for national and regional digital policymaking, informing the development of results-oriented tools, such as eT Ready action plans and e-commerce strategies, grounded in multi-stakeholder consultations and aligned with broader development goals.

To support countries in translating diagnostics into specific action, UNCTAD offers ongoing technical assistance through its eTrade Implementation Support Mechanism. The Mechanism facilitates multi-stakeholder coordination, strengthens policy dialogue and aligns development partner efforts at national and regional levels. That hands-on, results-oriented support helps countries turn digital ambitions into measurable progress and enhance their integration into the global digital economy. Implementation reviews are a core component of the Mechanism. They are essential for tracking progress, identifying persistent gaps and documenting good practices and policy impacts. Since 2020, those reviews have also contributed to tailored support for reform and the emergence of a dynamic network of eTrade focal points – mid-level government officials who drive reform efforts and engage stakeholders across sectors.

Building policymaking capacity is a central priority in that effort. In May 2024, a capacity-building workshop for eTrade focal points featured thematic sessions and peer learning on digital trade provisions in trade agreements and national e-commerce marketplaces. It also included hands-on training on the eTrade Reform Tracker, a digital tool launched in 2024 to monitor reform implementation in real time. Discussions highlighted the continued need for targeted capacity-building, particularly for least developed countries, and reinforced the importance of collaborative efforts, such as the Implementation Support Mechanism and the eTrade for all initiative, for "connecting the dots" between Governments, development partners and donors.

The urgency of strengthening digital readiness in developing countries has become increasingly prioritized at the global level. The Global Digital Compact was adopted in September 2024 as part of the Pact for the Future. It provides a global framework of principles and commitments to support an inclusive, secure and sustainable digital environment. Its implementation can be supported by various initiatives, including the eTrade for all initiative, which comprises 35 international partners. The present review adds value by offering a granular analysis of the quality of implementation processes of reforms enabling e-commerce, helping to foster better policy design, coordination and investment at national and regional levels.

Limited resources undermine e-commerce reform and governance efforts. Despite growing momentum in developing national and regional e-commerce frameworks, many countries continue to face significant constraints in advancing and implementing reforms due to limited human, technical and financial resources. Countries such as Fiji, Kenya, Trinidad and Tobago and Zambia have recently updated their e-commerce strategies, while others, including Peru, Rwanda and Senegal, are embedding e-commerce into their national development plans. Regional initiatives in the Economic Community of West African States, the East African Community and the Pacific Islands Forum have also made notable progress. Nevertheless, challenges such as weak political prioritization, institutional fragmentation and inadequate funding persist, often compounded by high staff turnover and limited technical capacity within implementing institutions and regional secretariats. While structured governance and monitoring mechanisms – such as interministerial committees and multi-stakeholder platforms – are emerging in countries such as Cambodia, Jordan and Vanuatu, their effectiveness is frequently undermined by resource constraints. Sustainable reform requires not only better coordination and inclusive stakeholder engagement at all levels but also long-term investments in capacity-building, digital tools and funding mechanisms. In that context, various UNCTAD initiatives, such as the eTrade Reform Tracker, are valuable resources for enhancing coordination, tracking progress and strengthening institutional capacity.

Strengthening evidence-based e-commerce policymaking through capacity-building is critical. The lack of statistical capabilities, inconsistent use of definitions and the dominance of informal, mobile-based commerce limit the availability of reliable and comparable statistics measuring e-commerce and digital trade. That calls for greater international cooperation, for example through the UNCTAD task group on measuring e-commerce value, which is developing global guidelines to support capacity-building. To bridge that information gap, Peru, Rwanda, Senegal and Tunisia are among countries currently developing national observatories, data collection tools and consumer barometers to generate useful market insights and track consumer behaviour and the industry trends of e-commerce and digital platforms. Overall, however, partner countries are increasingly calling for more sustained capacity-building to strengthen statistical capacity and foster data-driven policymaking in the digital economy.

B. Main developments in national and regional e-commerce ecosystems

While global Internet access continues to expand, significant disparities persist, especially in least developed countries and landlocked developing countries. Infrastructure gaps, high data costs and limited digital literacy remain critical barriers to digital inclusion. To address those challenges, partner countries are implementing large-scale connectivity projects. National initiatives, such as the fibre optic roll-out in Côte d'Ivoire and the Digital Acceleration Project in Malawi, exemplify targeted efforts to improve last-mile connectivity and digital service delivery. In the Pacific region, new submarine cable deployments are improving access and reliability across the island States. Those efforts are further supported by satellite-based technologies, providing flexible and resilient connectivity solutions, which are vital in disaster-prone or remote areas. Improved Internet access is also driving the expansion of digital services in critical sectors, such as finance, agriculture and public administration.

Modernizing logistics infrastructure and transport networks is key to improving last-mile delivery and cross-border e-commerce. Countries are leveraging digital tools, such as the Global Positioning System, artificial intelligence (AI) and the Internet of things, as well as the wide postal infrastructure, to optimize supply chains and foster trade inclusion in remote and rural areas, while prioritizing environmentally sustainable logistics. Regional initiatives, such as upgraded customs systems and trade corridors in East Africa, are expected to streamline trade flows and reduce transaction costs. Meanwhile, paperless trade remains a bottleneck in many places, signalling the need for further digital integration.

The rapid expansion of mobile money and digital payment platforms is transforming financial ecosystems in developing regions. Interoperable systems, real-time settlements and cross-border payment solutions are accelerating financial inclusion and boosting e-commerce participation. Cambodia, Kenya and Rwanda are implementing robust digital finance strategies, while regional platforms such as the Pan-African Payment and Settlement System (PAPSS), are paving the way for integrated intra-African payments.

To foster trust and inclusiveness, Governments are reforming legal and regulatory frameworks for e-commerce, data protection and cybersecurity. Progress is evident in several regions, including East Africa and the Pacific, where harmonization efforts and updated laws are creating safer digital environments. Emerging technologies, such as AI, are also prompting new governance, as seen in newly adopted national strategies on AI in Kenya, Mauritania and Zambia.

Digital literacy and skills development are fundamental to inclusive digital growth. Countries are embedding digital education in school curricula, expanding vocational training and supporting youth entrepreneurship. Public-private partnerships and innovation hubs are playing a vital role in equipping individuals and MSMEs with the tools to participate in the digital economy. Initiatives in Kenya, Senegal and the Solomon Islands, among others, reflect that growing momentum.

Despite increased digital activity, access to early-stage capital remains a major constraint. Partner countries are addressing that through start-up acts, innovation funds and regional investment initiatives. Programmes such as the Timbuktoo initiative of the United Nations Development Programme and national ventures in Bangladesh and Mauritania are all aimed at bridging financing gaps and catalysing innovation. Continued progress will depend on policy coherence, regulatory reform and ecosystem support.

Chapter I

Improving policymaking to foster a thriving e-commerce environment

The eTrade Readiness Assessments (eT Readies) of UNCTAD have catalysed the development of action plans and e-commerce strategies in more than 40 developing countries and contributed to regional frameworks, especially in Africa and the Pacific. Those tools also help countries align national and regional efforts with global commitments enshrined in the Global Digital Compact, which promotes an open, free, secure and inclusive digital future for all. As digital trade becomes central to economic development, coherent and coordinated policy approaches across national, regional and global levels are increasingly relevant.

The countries and regions reviewed in the present report are progressing at varying speeds. Many of them face limited high-level political endorsement, weak institutional capacity, insufficient financing and fragmented development partner support, which together hinder sustained reform efforts. While some countries and regions have established governance and monitoring systems to coordinate the implementation of relevant reforms, others struggle with coordination and continuity. Leveraging UNCTAD tools, such as the eTrade Reform Tracker, can enhance collaboration, monitoring and knowledge-sharing. Strengthening evidence-based policymaking, inclusive institutional frameworks and long-term capacity-building will be critical to ensure impactful and sustained digital trade reforms.

A. Sustained support and partnerships of the United Nations Conference on Trade and Development for advancing digital economy reforms

UNCTAD plays a critical role in supporting countries and regions in moving steadily from assessments to implementation of digital economy reforms. More than 40 eTrade Readies have been conducted, mostly benefiting least developed countries, landlocked developing countries and small island developing States. The methodology of the reviews has also proven adaptable to more advanced developing contexts, with Indonesia becoming the first G20 country to benefit from the tailored assistance of UNCTAD in this area. The approach taken advocates for a whole-of-government and multi-stakeholder model, fostering public-private dialogue and forging partnerships with development actors to help scale national efforts. Building on the capacities developed through the eT Ready process, 15 countries have developed short-term operational tools, such as an eT Ready action plan, to more medium-term, more comprehensive, nationally owned and holistic policy tools, such as a national e-commerce strategy or policy with the technical support of UNCTAD (figure I).

Figure 1
eT Readies and e-commerce strategies, action plans and policies (as at July 2025)

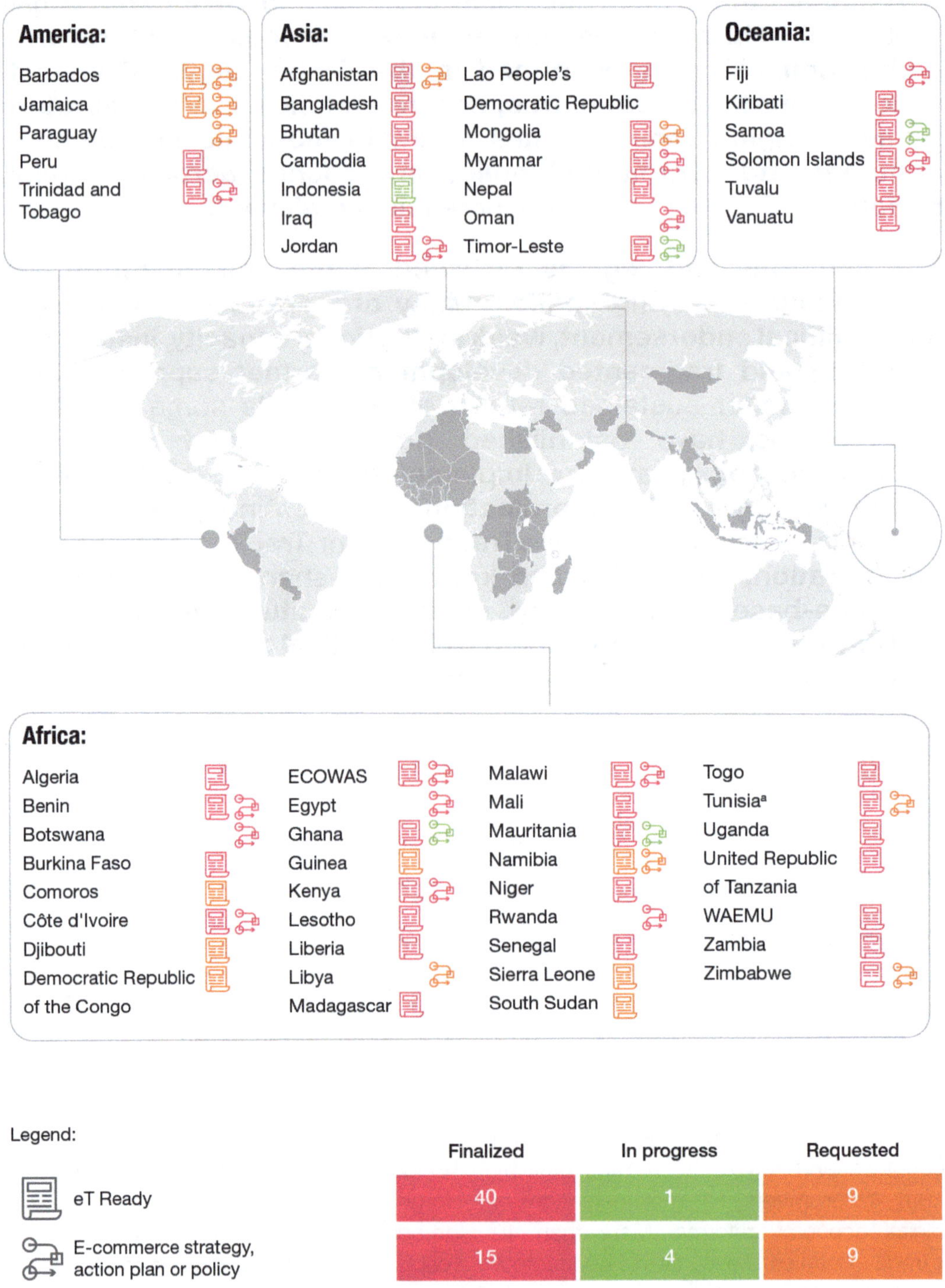

Source: Compiled by UNCTAD.
[a] An action plan has been developed and an e-commerce strategy has been requested.

Advancing digital economy reforms requires not only sustained technical support but also strong partnerships and collaboration among Governments, development partners, the private sector and civil society. The ongoing role of UNCTAD in facilitating multi-stakeholder cooperation and aligning efforts across national and regional levels is critical to overcoming challenges and ensuring inclusive, coordinated progress in digital transformation.

The need for deepening multi-stakeholder collaboration and international cooperation in the digital domain has gained unprecedented prominence. The present review echoes and amplifies the outcomes of the seventh session of the Intergovernmental Group of Experts on E-commerce and the Digital Economy, held from 6 to 8 May 2024, in Geneva. During that session, the Group of Experts emphasized the urgency of strengthening digital readiness in developing countries, especially in the face of cascading global crises and widening digital divides. It highlighted the uneven impacts of digitalization and the persistent barriers many countries faced, including gender and urban/rural divides, as well as rising concerns, such as the environmental impact of digitalization,[1] and challenges in navigating data governance and platform dominance. It adopted a set of agreed policy recommendations, calling for stronger collaboration between the international community and development partners with the aim of bolstering the capacities of countries to design, implement, coordinate and monitor progress on e-commerce enabling reform measures, using tools that were tailored to each country's needs, while ensuring inclusivity and equitable access to benefits for all, including women, youth and vulnerable groups.[2]

Those principles are also central to the Global Digital Compact, a landmark multilateral initiative adopted by the General Assembly in September 2024 as part of the Pact for the Future. In the Compact, the General Assembly outlined a set of principles and commitments fostering an inclusive, secure and sustainable digital environment, objective 2 of which is particularly relevant in the context of the present review. The Compact recognizes that advancing digital inclusion requires a predictable and transparent enabling environment that encompasses policy, legal and regulatory frameworks that support innovation, protect consumer rights, nurture digital talent and skills, promote fair competition and digital entrepreneurship, and enhance consumer confidence and trust in the digital economy. It provides a comprehensive framework and holistic approach for digital cooperation and governance, at international and national levels, that can help enhance productivity, facilitate the growth of e-commerce, improve competitiveness, accelerate digital transformation and support investments.

The need for deepening multi-stakeholder collaboration and international cooperation in the digital domain has gained unprecedented momentum.

1 Informed by UNCTAD (2024a) (see box 4 below), this topic was the focus of the eighth session of the Intergovernmental Group of Experts on E-commerce and the Digital Economy: https://unctad.org/meeting/intergovernmental-group-experts-e-commerce-and-digital-economy-8th-session. The environmental implications of the rise of e-commerce and the digital economy are an important element in UNCTAD research and intergovernmental work and were recently included in its capacity-building activities. The eT Ready of Indonesia, started in 2025, marks the first time that the environmental impact of e-commerce and digital trade is explicitly included in an assessment.

2 UNCTAD (2024b).

Table 1
Objectives and focus areas outlined in the Global Digital Compact

Objectives	Focus areas
1. Close all digital divides and accelerate progress across the Sustainable Development Goals	• Connectivity • Digital literacy, skills and capacities • Digital public goods and digital public infrastructure
2. Expand inclusion in and benefits from the digital economy for all	• Enabling environments for digital transformation • Knowledge-sharing and technology transfer • Capacity-building
3 Foster an inclusive, open, safe and secure digital space that respects, protects and promotes human rights	• Human rights • Internet governance • Digital trust and safety • Information integrity
4. Advance responsible, equitable and interoperable data governance approaches	• Data privacy and security • Data for the Sustainable Development Goals and for development • Cross-border data flows • Interoperable data governance
5. Enhance international governance of AI for the benefit of humanity	• Governance of AI

Source: UNCTAD, based on the official text of the Global Digital Compact.

The success of such a framework depends heavily on enhanced partnerships and collaborative efforts. UNCTAD will play an active role in facilitating the implementation of the Compact. Together with the United Nations Industrial Development Organization, it will co-lead the implementation of commitments under objective 2 and, together with the United Nations University, those under objective 4. That effort builds on and integrates existing initiatives, including those linked to the World Summit on the Information Society and the UNCTAD-led eTrade for all initiative (box 1).

Box 1
Advancing cooperation through the eTrade for all initiative

Launched in 2016, the eTrade for all initiative exemplifies the power of partnerships, bringing together 35 international organizations, regional development banks, civil society entities and national agencies as partners committed to advancing digital inclusion in developing countries. It actively supports objectives 1 and 2 (para. 21 (d)) of the Global Digital Compact by facilitating multi-stakeholder technical assistance and knowledge-sharing. Its platform (etradeforall.org) provides a rich resource of news, events, capacity-building courses and research on e-commerce and the digital economy.

eTrade for all partners continue to be actively involved in various UNCTAD capacity-building activities, especially in the development and implementation of eT Readies and e-commerce strategies. In 2024, 22 partners engaged in various UNCTAD-led activities, including 13 partners supporting eT Readies, e-commerce strategies and their implementation, 9 contributing to eTrade for Women activities and 12 being involved in research, analysis and measurement.

Source: UNCTAD (2025a).

The eTrade Implementation Support Mechanism provides a unique engagement platform for partner countries to build policymaking capacities for e-commerce. Implementation reviews have constituted a cornerstone of the Mechanism since 2020. They have helped to calibrate the level of support required to assist partner countries, as they move forward in implementing reforms and initiatives enabling e-commerce. Through continuous engagement with stakeholders, particularly eTrade focal points,[3] UNCTAD has contributed to shaping a community of e-commerce policy practitioners who are championing national implementation processes, primarily by actively engaging with public and private sector stakeholders. The eTrade focal points regularly benefit from tailored capacity-building workshops (figure II) and participation in global forums, such as UNCTAD eWeek and the Intergovernmental Group of Experts on E-commerce and the Digital Economy. The reviews and the eTrade capacity-building workshops have proven instrumental in designing support initiatives and facilitating knowledge- and experience-sharing across countries and regional groups.

The eTrade capacity-building workshop organized in conjunction with the seventh session of the Intergovernmental Group of Experts on E-commerce and the Digital Economy brought together 28 focal points from partner countries and regional economic communities across Africa, Asia and the Pacific and Latin America and the Caribbean, underscoring the growing demand for peer learning and South-South collaboration. On that occasion, participants addressed topics such as digital trade agreements and e-commerce marketplaces and benefited from presentations from several eTrade for all partners, including the Diplo Foundation, the International Trade Centre (ITC), the Economic Commission for Latin America and the Caribbean, the World Trade Organization (WTO), as well as other organizations, such as the United Nations Development Programme (UNDP). The workshop also provided the opportunity to organize a hands-on simulation exercise of the eTrade Reform Tracker, inaugurating its roll-out phase in requesting partner countries (box 2).

Among the main messages that emerged from the discussions was that multi-stakeholder partnerships were essential to support the political leadership and national stakeholders in their efforts to integrate and benefit from the new global digital economy. That points to the continued need to "connect the dots" among beneficiary countries, partners and donors in order to foster inclusive e-commerce development frameworks at national and regional levels.

UNCTAD has contributed to shaping a community of policy practitioners who are championing the implementation of reforms and initiatives enabling e-commerce.

[3] These are mainly senior government officials from trade ministries or other entities recognized for their leadership in e-commerce. Since the first eT Ready stocktaking exercise in 2019, UNCTAD has strived to maintain and strengthen relationships with these focal points as part of its follow-up efforts. When officials transition out of their roles, UNCTAD continues to build new connections, often with the support of the Geneva-based Permanent Missions of their respective countries.

Figure 2
Capacity-building in action – feedback from eTrade focal points

"The eT Ready study is the only evaluation of e-commerce in Tunisia. It has helped identify priorities for reform, reinforcing the coherence of national policies, the country's position in regional discussions and access to political and technical support."

Khabbab Hadhri, Director of E-commerce Development, Ministry of Trade and Export Development, Tunisia.

"The eT Ready for Senegal identified national priorities, particularly useful in the context of the negotiations of the AfCFTA [African Continental Free Trade Area] Digital Trade Protocol. It also highlighted measures to address certain sectoral gaps."

Fara Makha Diop, Head of the E-commerce Promotion Office, Ministry of Industry and Trade, Senegal.

"The eT Ready greatly helped the country participate in regional and international e-commerce initiatives, including in the AfCFTA context. Participation in the eTrade capacity-building workshop (May 2024) enabled Mauritania to identify best practices and the most strategic areas of cooperation for its development."

Matchiane Bacar, Adviser, Ministry of Digital Transformation, Innovation and Modernization of the Administration, Mauritania.

"I will definitely apply the knowledge acquired from attending the eTrade Reform Tracker live demonstration. As a starting point, I will share the presentations with other stakeholders in Zambia. I will also share information on the Tracker, a useful tool for tracking and monitoring implementation of e-commerce strategic objectives."

Michelo Makwembo, Senior Economist, Ministry of Commerce, Trade and Industry, Zambia.

"The eT Ready carried out in 2017 with UNCTAD support was a key milestone for e-commerce development in Cambodia. In addition to providing a diagnostic, the eT Ready charted a future road map for further growth of the e-commerce ecosystem. The eT Ready continues to be a key source to situate our current needs in the context of global trends in digital policy developments."

Laichea Chea, Director of International Cooperation, Ministry of Commerce, Cambodia.

"The eT Ready report enabled more structured dialogue in the Solomon Islands between government agencies, the private sector and international bodies, strengthening multi-stakeholder engagement through the establishment of an e-commerce steering committee. It also enhanced participation in regional forums, including the Pacific E-commerce Initiative led by the Pacific Islands Forum, aligning the country's efforts with the Pacific Regional E-commerce Strategy and Roadmap."

Richard Nokia, Director E-commerce Implementation Unit, Ministry of Commerce, Industry, Labour and Immigration, Solomon Islands.

"The eT Ready increased the capacity of Tuvalu to generate policy cooperation and development support but there is still a need to train staff across various government departments. Some issues faced by our technical officers include understaffing, heavy workloads are assigned to a small number of employees, leaving insufficient time for the respective officers to focus on developing policies and to benefit from skills training."

Toaiga Semisi, Director of Trade, Department of Trade, Tuvalu.

B. Advancing national and regional e-commerce development frameworks to accelerate e-commerce reforms

Building on the momentum generated by the continued engagement of UNCTAD and the growing recognition of the importance of inclusive digital transformation, countries are increasingly translating diagnostic insights into structured policy responses. The emergence of national and regional e-commerce strategies, policies and action plans, as well as overall digital economy strategies, reflects a deepening commitment to advance coherent e-commerce frameworks at different levels. However, progress also reveals the complexity of implementation of policy reforms in diverse institutional and developmental contexts. As Governments seek to align national priorities with regional and global digital agendas, understanding how those frameworks are designed, adopted and operationalized becomes essential. In the present section of the review, focus is on how countries and regions are advancing e-commerce development frameworks, the challenges encountered and the role of regional cooperation in reinforcing national reform efforts.

1. National e-commerce frameworks

Across Africa and the Pacific, eT Readies have played a catalytic role in shaping national e-commerce frameworks. Since the third review, a growing number of countries, primarily in Africa and the Pacific, have developed or finalized national e-commerce strategies, policies and actions plans. Countries stress the importance of aligning digital transformation efforts with national development goals. National e-commerce strategies, policies and action plans are seen as key policymaking tools to facilitate collaboration across sectors, prioritize investments and raise the profile of e-commerce in national development planning. Those developments reaffirm the continued relevance of eT Readies as essential tools for shaping comprehensive and inclusive national e-commerce frameworks. The following serve to illustrate the point:

- Malawi launched its eT Ready Action Plan in March 2025. As one of the main actions identified in the Plan, an e-commerce policy and strategy will be developed with the support of the African Development Bank, to frame an overarching strategic vision for e-commerce development.
- The National E-commerce Strategy 2023 of Kenya was launched in Nairobi in December 2023 by both the Ministers of Information, Communications and the Digital Economy and Trade, Investments and Industry, supported by UNCTAD and the German Agency for International Cooperation (GIZ).[4]

© GIZ | Officials with copies of the National E-commerce Strategy 2023 of Kenya during its launch in Nairobi.

- The National E-commerce Strategy (2023–2027) of Zambia, developed by the Ministry of Commerce, Trade and Industry, was launched in December 2023.[5]

[4] See https://unctad.org/news/kenya-unveils-e-commerce-strategy-better-harness-digital-economy.
[5] See https://www.mcti.gov.zm/wp-content/uploads/2024/01/National-E-Commerce-Strategy-2023.pdf.

- In the Pacific, Fiji is the fifth and latest member of the Pacific Islands Forum (PIF), after Samoa, Solomon Islands, Tonga and Vanuatu, to have developed a national e-commerce strategy. Its National E-commerce Strategy (2025–2029) was launched in February 2025 and was developed by the Ministry of Trade, Co-operatives, Micro, Small and Medium Enterprises and Communications in collaboration with UNCTAD, with support from Australia, the European Union and New Zealand through the Pacific Digital Economy Programme.[6]

Some strategies formulated prior to 2020 are starting to become obsolete or poorly aligned with the current digital and policy landscape. The recovery after the coronavirus disease (COVID-19) pandemic, the evolution of the global digital economy and rising geopolitical tensions have exposed new vulnerabilities,[7] especially among least developed countries, highlighting the need for updated frameworks. For example, Trinidad and Tobago launched a new national e-commerce strategy in March 2025, with support from UNCTAD, building on its 2017–2021 e-commerce strategy and informed by its eT Ready prepared in 2024. Trinidad and Tobago has made substantial progress in the development of its e-commerce strategies, marked by significant advancements and refinements between the past and present policy frameworks. The earlier strategy was focused on foundational infrastructure and regulatory frameworks, while digital transformation, inclusivity and global competitiveness are emphasized in the 2025–2030 strategy. Also, while the previous strategy was focused on four key actions, the 2025–2030 strategy contains a detailed implementation plan with four strategic goals, 15 objectives and 42 measures.

The Government of Senegal, recognizing the shortcomings in the implementation of the national digital strategy (Digital Senegal Strategy 2016–2025) and with the intention to keep abreast of the latest global and regional trends, introduced an ambitious New Technological Deal in February 2025,[8] aimed at positioning the country as a digital powerhouse in Africa.

With growing recognition of e-commerce as a driver of economic development, the area is increasingly integrated into national and sectoral development agendas. Mainstreaming helps align policy actions across areas such as education, financial inclusion and payments, private sector development, e-commerce and digital trade, as a lever for economic transformation and trade diversification. Examples of such an evolution include initiatives in Nepal, Peru, Rwanda and Senegal:

- In Nepal, digital literacy and financial inclusion measures from its National Strategy on Development and Use of E-commerce, developed in 2019 as a follow-up to the eT Ready, were integrated into the Financial Sector Development Strategy (2023). Digital trade is prioritized under its Trade Integration Strategy (2023) and the new Commerce Policy adopted in 2025.
- In Peru, in the Digital Economy Articulating Programme, approved in April 2024 as part of the National Digital Transformation Policy for 2030, e-commerce is identified as a key pillar with 70 per cent of the measures established in the National Competitiveness and Productivity Plan 2024 linked to digital transformation.
- In Rwanda, the National Strategy for Transformation 2024–2029[9] contains

6 See https://pacificecommerce.org/fiji-launches-national-e-commerce-strategy-to-drive-digital-transformation-and-economic-growth.

7 In her report to the sixteenth session of the Conference, the Secretary-General of UNCTAD highlighted the major trends that were reshaping the world, which include: the emergence of a multipolar global economy, rapid technological transformation, the escalating triple planetary crisis, demographic changes and urbanization. An advance copy is available at: https://unctad.org/system/files/official-document/osginf2024d7_en.pdf.

8 See https://www.newdealtechnologique.sn (in French).

9 See https://www.minecofin.gov.rw/index.php?eID=dumpFile&t=f&f=112653&token=dbe8e7d0faf00f43ce4605a42bfaa0fd795a5bb8.

an e-commerce readiness programme under its economic transformation pillar to help micro-, small and medium-sized enterprises (MSMEs) leverage digital trade platforms for exports.

- In Senegal, several ministries and implementing agencies have integrated some of the actions of its 2019 national e-commerce development strategy into operational plans, including tax reforms and e-procurement measures aligned with specific actions contained in the strategy.

Despite rising interest in e-commerce development, many countries still face a dual challenge: the absence of sustained high-level political endorsement and persistent operational capacity gaps. Translating e-commerce strategies, policies or action plans into specific reforms remains challenging. Top-down, e-commerce is not consistently positioned as a political or economic priority, which weakens the commitment to institutionalize and implement reforms. Bottom-up, the institutions responsible for designing and implementing e-commerce reforms are frequently underresourced and face technical and institutional limitations, such as understaffing or high turnover rates, limiting their ability to address complex and fast-evolving digital issues. Those challenges are compounded by overlapping institutional mandates, which can lead to fragmented responsibilities and make coordination difficult. Insufficient dialogue between the public and private sectors further undermines momentum.

Sustaining political leadership and ensuring effective interministerial coordination are areas in which the countries reviewed most often struggle. As a result, the preparation and validation of strategies can become lengthy and the risk of losing momentum, especially after Governments transition, is high. Without formal endorsement at the highest level, it becomes difficult to galvanize the support needed to drive e-commerce reforms. Delays also limit the possibilities of aligning with the programming cycles of donors and development partners, which often require a sustained dialogue and a longer-term planning horizon. The experiences of several countries illustrate how those challenges play out in practice, with varying degrees of progress and institutional engagement.

For example, in Benin, an e-commerce strategy was developed in 2021 but never officially endorsed. In Côte d'Ivoire a national e-commerce strategy was developed between 2023 and 2024 in collaboration with UNCTAD; however, an action plan covering the period 2025–2028 is still pending adoption. In Ghana, political changes in 2024 delayed the validation of the e-commerce strategy and an established committee was recently reconstituted with new nominations. In Kiribati and Tuvalu, e-commerce policies and strategies were drafted but are still awaiting formal approval by the cabinet. Papua New Guinea validated its national e-commerce strategy and road map in June 2024, but they have not yet been approved.

> Country efforts in driving e-commerce reforms are constrained by weak political endorsement and operational capacity gaps.

At the same time, there is no one-size-fits-all framework to apply. Countries adopt different mixes of strategies, policies and action plans, depending on their legal traditions, governance models, institutional capacity, sectoral priorities and reform ambitions. E-commerce development is a relatively new area for policymaking and global trends are playing an increasing role in accelerating reforms. Thereby, Governments can be confronted with tough choices and require a more solid and articulated nexus between government vision, policy directions and actionability of reforms.

In Kenya, Rwanda[10] and Samoa, although e-commerce strategies were developed first, the need for an overarching e-commerce policy became evident later. Such policies were necessary to fully enable the implementation of the

[10] With UNCTAD support, the national e-commerce strategy in Rwanda was developed and published in March 2023 as an UNCTAD report.

The shrinking of external support for the financing of reforms enabling e-commerce may reverse recent gains in digital readiness.

e-commerce strategies, especially to drive legal and regulatory reforms. In Tunisia, two consecutive eT Ready action plans have been developed, but coordination among all stakeholders and effective engagement remains problematic. The eT Ready Action Plan is still considered a sectoral action plan developed by the Ministry of Commerce. To ensure the commitment of all ministerial entities, the development of a national e-commerce strategy is meant to ensure more effective involvement of all actors in their respective areas (e.g. payments, logistics and trade facilitation). The strategy/policy development and endorsement process, which typically includes comprehensive stakeholder consultations, approval by authoritative bodies and official publication confers on these documents a higher degree of stability and authority than that of a sectoral plan. While strategies and policies represent medium-term visions of the Government, aligned with national priorities, and aim to foster institutional coordination and continuity, sectoral plans, in contrast, promote a short-term, pragmatic approach that favours a flexible and iterative process.

The financing of reforms enabling e-commerce is still inadequate and constrained by limited institutional capacities. The present review confirms that financing of reforms enabling e-commerce remains insufficient, underscoring the urgent need to mobilize greater support. Limited prioritization of e-commerce reforms and weak capacity to convert priorities into fundable projects continue to undermine progress. Accurately estimating financing needs is challenging due to the cross-cutting nature of e-commerce and scattered budget lines across sectors.

Diversifying funding through partnerships anchored in national development cooperation frameworks is critical, especially considering the decline in official development assistance, which adds further pressure. While such assistance rose during the COVID-19 pandemic, current geopolitical shifts have led to an anticipated 20 per cent drop in aid budgets (UNCTAD, 2025b), which will likely affect the relatively modest ICT-related part of overall Aid-for-Trade flows. In 2023, commitments to the ICT sector hit a record high in absolute terms ($2.25 billion), yet they still made up just 3.5 per cent of total Aid for Trade, below the 4.1 per cent peak in 2021 (UNCTAD, 2025a).

For countries, especially least developed countries, already constrained by rising debt levels, that shrinking of external support may reverse recent gains in digital readiness. Strengthening domestic fiscal strategies, including through indirect taxation of domestic and cross-border e-commerce, can help increase resource availability.[11] For example, during the review, the Government of Senegal reported allocating domestic resources to improve the fiscal regime in the digital economy, including value added tax regulations for online sales and foreign service providers of digital services.[12]

At the level of the United Nations, instruments such as the recently launched digital transformation window of the Joint Sustainable Development Goals Fund are helping to align digital priorities with the objectives of the Sustainable Development Goals. Country initiatives are led by resident coordinators' offices and implemented by various United Nations entities, in partnership with private sector and development partners to foster a thriving digital ecosystem. For example, in Kenya, the Digital Platforms Kenya (DigiKen) project, launched in October 2024,[13] supports the development of local digital platforms to drive inclusive

[11] A recent study by UNCTAD (2025c) can help to understand the significant implications and challenges of e-commerce and digital trade for taxation authorities, based on the policies put in place by several countries.

[12] Order No. 034269/MFB/DGID of 8 November 2023.

[13] The initiative is funded by the European Union and its member States. It is spearheaded by the Resident Coordinator and the Ministry of Information, Communications and the Digital Economy, and implemented by a consortium of United Nations entities. That consortium will collaborate with other development partners, such as GIZ Digital Transformation Center Kenya and the Estonian Centre for International Development.

sustainable social and economic progress. In Ghana, a new programme carried out by the United Nations Capital Development Fund (UNCDF), UNDP and UNCTAD is aimed at boosting the access of MSMEs to finance, digital skills and e-commerce,[14] with UNCTAD supporting policy reform with an e-commerce strategy and the eTrade Reform Tracker to coordinate the implementation of the national e-commerce strategy.

In summary, resource mobilization efforts must be more coordinated, inclusive and transparent, to reduce fragmentation, avoid duplication and maximize impact. Development partners can go a long way in enabling sustainable solutions, for example by operating a shift from short-term projects to long-term capacity-building and resource mobilization strategies. That could include:

- Empowering local institutional and human resources and investing in training programmes, digital skills development and public sector capacity to design and implement policies.
- Providing predictable and flexible financing, moving away from fragmented, one-off project funding and establishing multi-year, funding mechanisms that support national e-commerce strategies aligned with development goals.
- Supporting coordination across ministries and institutions and strengthening multi-stakeholder governance mechanisms that bring together key players across the e-commerce ecosystem, including public and private sector institutions.

Inclusive stakeholder engagement and subnational participation are essential in advancing effective and sustainable e-commerce reforms. Building stronger institutional anchoring and policy visibility, and stakeholder engagement through public-private dialogue and awareness-raising, is essential to ensure broad-based support for e-commerce reforms. Educating stakeholders about the benefits and challenges of e-commerce and digital trade is essential for building trust, highlighting successful initiatives and good practices and strengthening commitment to implementation. Inclusive multi-stakeholder participation, including that of women, youth and persons with disabilities,[15] contributes to more balanced and effective reforms. UNCTAD-supported processes increasingly reflect that approach, including through synergies with initiatives such as eTrade for Women,[16] which is aimed at promoting the voice of women digital entrepreneurs in policymaking. In line with that trend, several countries have established dedicated platforms to facilitate dialogue and inclusive engagement in the development and implementation of e-commerce policies:

- The Digital Trade Week (March 2025) in Mongolia brought together more than 70 public and private sector representatives from the digital trade industry, promoting women and youth participation in digital trade and addressing logistics and digital payment challenges faced by MSMEs, start-ups and rural businesses in e-commerce and digital trade. It was co-organized by the Ministry of Foreign Affairs, the Economic and Social Commission for Asia and the Pacific and the European Union-funded International Trade Development in Mongolia Project.[17]

[14] The approximately $3 million three-year programme (2024–2027) is supported by the European Union and other key States. It is expected to boost the productivity of approximately 25,000 MSMEs, primarily those led by youth and women. The programme is being implemented jointly by UNCDF, UNDP and UNCTAD under the auspices of the Resident Coordinator and the Ministry of Trade, Agribusiness and Industry and in collaboration with key stakeholders.

[15] This has recently been done in the preparation of the eT Readies and e-commerce strategies developed for the Economic Community of West African States and Kenya (see annex I), as well as in Fiji, Timor-Leste and Trinidad and Tobago (finalized in 2025).

[16] See https://etradeforall.org/et4women.

[17] For more information, see https://www.gov.mn/en/news/all/aea666e1-1318-4410-ba58-f12fae9d8883 and https://www.unescap.org/events/2025/mongolias-digital-trade-week.

- Following similar experiences in Burkina Faso and Togo, the Niger organized a first edition of its digital week in April 2024, gathering players from the public and private sectors, development partners, youth entrepreneurs, start-ups and financial technology (fintech) companies. The event offered a unique platform to exchange ideas, stimulate innovation and strengthen the understanding of the societal impact of digital technology.
- The E-commerce Symposium in Vanuatu, launched in 2021 and followed by annual editions, has provided a valuable forum for inclusive dialogue. The latest edition in May 2025 was held on the theme of “E-commerce, a driver of sustainable and inclusive economic growth in Vanuatu” (see annex I).

It is important that national and sectoral policies are integrated into local development plans to align them with community needs and foster balanced, country-wide digital development.

However, more efforts are needed to spearhead reforms enabling e-commerce at the subnational level. While national-level strategies have gained traction, subnational integration remains limited. To ensure that e-commerce expands beyond urban areas, it is important that national and sectoral policies are integrated into local development plans. Integration at the subnational level starts with a more active participation of stakeholders beyond the capital. That can include involving local administrators from smaller cities and administrative departments in multi-stakeholder engagement processes, in the context of the development and implementation of national e-commerce strategies and policies. Such engagement helps align national reforms with local needs and fosters more balanced digital development across the country. Kenya provides an interesting case in which the Department for Trade engaged with the county governments, through the Council of Governors, in the preparation and implementation of the National E-commerce Strategy. That approach offers a valuable model for early and sustained subnational level involvement.

Digital solutions are leveraged for public engagement and more inclusive policymaking. E-participation, using digital tools to engage citizens in policy processes, is gaining ground to make e-commerce and digital economy policies more inclusive, transparent and trusted. It enables broad public input, helping Governments design better-informed and widely supported policies. E-participation, as defined by the Department of Economic and Social Affairs, is about fostering civic engagement and open, participatory governance through ICT. Among the countries reviewed, Mongolia, Peru and Rwanda are in the top 50 positions of the E-Participation Index (2024), a supplementary index to the United Nations E-Government Survey.[18]

Notable examples of e-participation tools used in policymaking processes related to e-commerce and the digital economy are the Tawasal and Participa Perú platforms in Jordan and Peru, respectively:[19]

- The Tawasal platform was used for public consultations on the Digital Inclusion Policy and Implementation Plan 2025 and the ex ante regulatory impact assessment on the regulation of e-commerce, in 2024, addressing fairness in the digital market, among other things.
- The Participa Perú platform enabled more than 14,000 citizens and experts

[18] Followed by Jordan, Ghana and Kenya in seventieth, eighty-second and eighty-fourth positions, respectively, out of the 193 countries surveyed. The purpose of Index is not to prescribe any specific practice, but rather to offer insight into how different countries are using online tools in promoting interaction between the Government and its people, as well as among the people, for the benefit of all.

[19] Tawasal (https://www.tawasal.gov.jo) serves as a unified public consultation tool, enabling dialogue between government agencies, individuals, non-governmental organizations and stakeholders, including discussions on policies related to e-commerce. It facilitates consultations on government legislation and projects before their adoption and approval, ensuring the inclusive participation of all segments of society in government decision-making processes. Participa Perú (https://www.gob.pe/participa) is an online space to listen to the proposals of all citizens to achieve the country’s objectives. It is the first result of the Government and Digital Transformation Laboratory, which allows the direct participation of civil society, the public and private sectors, academia and citizens at large.

to co-design the National Digital Transformation Policy for 2030. It was approved in 2023 and covers topics such as education, the economy, connectivity, government, data, security and talent.

2. Regional e-commerce frameworks

Regional cooperation has emerged as both supported by, and a powerful driver to accelerate, the implementation of national reforms enabling e-commerce. Feedback received from countries reinforced findings from previous reviews. National eT Readies, action plans, strategies and policies are recognized as important tools to prepare countries for meaningful involvement in regional e-commerce initiatives. Regional initiatives can range from actions with a more voluntary nature, such as policies and strategies, to binding commitments embedded in trade agreements with e-commerce chapters. Regional e-commerce strategies are increasingly valued for their ability to secure high-level, sustained support for national e-commerce development initiatives, while enabling reforms to be pursued in a more coordinated, cost-effective and efficient way. Those strategies provide a framework to identify and align priority areas, facilitate peer learning and knowledge exchange, coordinate implementation efforts among member States and track progress, as well as support resource mobilization efforts and engagement with development partners more effectively.

Regional organizations, such as the East African Community (EAC), the Economic Community of West African States (ECOWAS) and PIF, have recognized the critical role of UNCTAD in building the foundations for their regional e-commerce strategies. Those strategies are reinforcing and complementing national e-commerce reforms, even as they face different implementation challenges.

- EAC adopted its E-commerce Strategy in July 2022, building, inter alia, on eT Readies conducted in Kenya, Uganda and the United Republic of Tanzania. Since then, the EAC secretariat has worked closely with member States to build a conducive environment for its implementation. Legal reform was prioritized, with progress made in the areas of e-transaction legislation and consumer protection (see chap. II, sect. D). An E-commerce Engagement Platform was officially launched in May 2025, bringing together various representatives of the regional e-commerce ecosystem. However, the EAC secretariat faces challenges in aligning regional and national stakeholder platforms and ensuring consistent engagement, which are crucial for effective monitoring (see sect. C below).
- ECOWAS adopted its Regional E-commerce Strategy in July 2023, marking a key step towards advancing digital trade in the region.[20] Since then, implementation has progressed slowly due to limited financial resources and coordination challenges. However, it has gained momentum following the official launch of the Regional E-commerce Committee in July 2025 and the approval of its terms of reference, alongside other initiatives aimed at promoting the inclusion of women, youth and persons with disabilities in the e-commerce ecosystem. As the strategy implementation moves forward, enhanced communication and awareness-raising will be essential to ensure that stakeholders at all levels are informed, engaged and focused on its objectives.

Regional e-commerce strategies are increasingly valued for their ability to secure high-level, sustained support for national e-commerce development initiatives.

[20] Aligned with ECOWAS Vision 2050, the Regional E-commerce Strategy contains three key goals: institutional strengthening, securing trust, and e-commerce intelligence and inclusion. It responds to the needs of ECOWAS, identified in the regional assessment prepared by UNCTAD (2022b).

© ECOWAS | Officials meeting in Lagos, Nigeria, in July 2025 for the launch of the Regional E-commerce Committee and Joint ECOWAS-UNCTAD eTrade for Women workshop.

- PIF launched its Regional E-commerce Strategy and Roadmap in 2021. The development of eT Readies and other e-commerce assessments following UNCTAD methodology played a foundational role in developing the regional and various national e-commerce strategies. That has fostered a sound regional e-commerce development framework, reflecting both local needs and regional digital ambitions, laying the foundations for the region's digital transformation efforts (see annex I). The PIF secretariat has since established a well-articulated implementation architecture[21] and monitoring system under the umbrella of its Pacific E-commerce Initiative (see sect. C below).

Another important regional framework that is relevant for the countries reviewed is the Association of Southeast Asian Nations (ASEAN) Digital Economy Framework Agreement, which is built on the ASEAN Agreement on Electronic Commerce. Negotiations began in 2023 and are expected to be concluded by December 2025.[22]

Regional e-commerce strategies can be a powerful catalyst for fostering implementation synergies and partnerships. By reinforcing the leadership role of regional organizations and promoting stronger ownership among member countries, those strategies help align priorities and coordinate efforts. They also provide opportunities to pool resources, establish regional financing mechanisms and attract both donor support and private investment, especially for capital-intensive areas such ICT infrastructure, digital payment systems and platforms. Experiences in the EAC and Pacific regions demonstrate how sustained and coordinated engagement with development partners can be strengthened through the implementation of regional e-commerce strategies:

- EAC has successfully leveraged its strategy to attract the support of development partners, aligning donor interventions with regional priorities.[23] Its annual Development Partners Forum and donor support matrix have improved transparency and coordination.
- In the Pacific region, the mobilization of partners led by PIF has resulted in $153 million of resources being allocated to support implementation of the strategy. Initiatives such as the Pacific E-commerce Alliance are moving in the right direction and can help to foster collaboration and reduce fragmentation. The launch of the Alliance in 2023, inspired by the eTrade for all initiative, created a regional network of partners to boost collaboration. Six partners have joined the initiative since its creation.

While the Pacific experience shows strong progress in harmonizing efforts at the national and regional levels, UNCTAD (2025d) underscored the need to avoid

[21] The Pacific E-commerce Committee was established in 2022 as the main governance and oversight mechanism, comprising government representatives acting as focal points from PIF member countries, as well as other stakeholders involved as observers in the implementation of the Strategy. It also includes two subcommittees, one for the private sector and one for development partners. It reports to the PIF Trade Ministers through the Steering Committee of the Pacific Aid-for-Trade Strategy Working Group.

[22] See https://asean.org/wp-content/uploads/2024/11/DEFA-Report-public-summary-expanded_Final_25112024.pdf.

[23] These include initiatives from the Team Europe Initiative of the European Union (Safe Digital Boost for Africa), GIZ (Pan-African E-commerce Initiative), the World Bank (Eastern Africa Regional Digital Integration Project), as well as TradeMark Africa support on e-payments.

overreliance on donor funding. Greater national and regional investment, budget prioritization and sustainable funding mechanisms are needed to strengthen ownership and ensure long-term sustainability of regional programmes.

Although eT Readies, e-commerce strategies and e-commerce policies have better equipped countries to engage in digital trade agreements, greater investment in capacity-building is needed. Such reference documents cover thematic areas, often included in such agreements. Feedback received from countries during the present review indicates that the reference documents were useful in support of policy discussions and engagement in the negotiation and implementation of trade agreements:

- Mongolia launched its fourth round of negotiations for an economic partnership agreement with the Republic of Korea in November 2024 and signed an interim free trade agreement with the Eurasian Economic Union during the fourth Eurasian Economic Forum held in June 2025, in Minsk. Both documents include e-commerce chapters.
- Peru used findings from its eT Ready to inform an Asia-Pacific economic cooperation report on MSME e-commerce practices and to support its accession process to the Organisation for Economic Co-operation and Development (OECD), for which e-commerce is a priority.
- Togo leveraged capacity-building from its eT Ready conducted in 2018 to actively engage in WTO discussions on e-commerce and the Information Technology Agreement and contribute to various editions of UNCTAD eWeek and sessions of the Intergovernmental Group of Experts on E-commerce and the Digital Economy.

Côte d'Ivoire, Senegal and other ECOWAS countries cited eT Readies and e-commerce strategies as instrumental in engaging with regional e-commerce initiatives and the AfCFTA Digital Trade Protocol. The Protocol is aimed at promoting intra-African digital trade, enhancing cooperation on digital matters among States Parties and creating a transparent, secure and trusted digital trade ecosystem. The implementation of the actions contained in the eT Readies and strategies can contribute to accelerating reforms aligned with the provisions of the Protocol. Moreover, countries that benefit from the eTrade Implementation Support Mechanism can also share good practices, engage in South-South experience-sharing and find solutions to common challenges as they move forward to implement the Protocol.

Despite that progress, feedback received during the review from various countries and regional organizations underscored the need for scaling up capacity-building efforts. Policymakers, negotiators and institutions must be equipped with the technical skills and strategic understanding required to navigate increasingly complex digital trade frameworks. That includes understanding issues such as cross-border data flows, e-commerce regulations, intellectual property rights and cybersecurity standards. Capacity-building not only ensures informed participation in negotiations but also enables countries to secure more equitable outcomes from multilateral trade agreements, implement commitments efficiently and leverage digital trade for sustainable economic growth. The following are some recent initiatives:

- Since 2022, the PIF secretariat has organized an annual "E-commerce rules course for policymakers" to build negotiation capacity in e-commerce laws and regulations. In early 2024, the most recent course strengthened the capacity of 30 government officials from the region to negotiate digital trade agreements and incorporate e-commerce provisions in future trade frameworks, enhancing their ability to engage effectively in global and regional e-commerce initiatives that are aligned

> By conducting eT Readies and adopting e-commerce strategies, countries have become better equipped to engage in regional e-commerce initiatives and negotiation of digital trade agreements, such as the AfCFTA Digital Trade Protocol.

with international best practices.[24]

- In 2024, the AfCFTA secretariat, in partnership with regional and international partners, conducted extensive workshops to support implementation of its founding agreement. A webinar series, entitled "E-commerce, trade and development: policy frameworks in Africa", brought together policymakers to discuss and assist with the implementation of the AfCFTA Digital Trade Protocol.[25] More recently, in May 2025, the AfCFTA Digital Trade Forum 2025 provided a platform for high-level dialogue, technical sessions and stakeholder engagement focused on operationalizing the Protocol. Not only did the Forum provide the opportunities for stakeholders present to unpack the Protocol's annexes and explore implementation pathways, it also allowed for detailed discussion on critical issues pertaining to cross-border data flows, digital payments, e-commerce regulation, cybersecurity and digital entrepreneurship.[26]

While those kinds of initiatives are welcome, training programmes should become more recurrent and integrated at the institutional level within lead agencies. They should be available in particular for members of national technical committees in charge of coordinating the implementation of e-commerce development reforms. Dedicated units in regional organizations that play a supportive role in the implementation of trade agreements (e.g. African regional economic communities in the AfCFTA context) should be resourced with adequate human and technical capacity to address the scope of digital trade issues. Effective monitoring systems are also needed to assess progress, identify capacity gaps and further inform training efforts. Effective capacity-building is crucial not only for informed negotiation but also for securing fairer outcomes and maximizing the development potential of digital trade.

C. Fostering effective multi-stakeholder governance mechanisms

Clear mandates, effective coordination and governance frameworks, as well as monitoring and evaluation systems and tools, are critical to drive effective and efficient implementation of e-commerce reforms.

The need for an articulated governance model is emerging to lead and coordinate the implementation of reforms. Countries and regions participating in the review have highlighted how developing clear mandates, establishing effective coordination and governance frameworks, as well as monitoring and evaluation systems and tools, are critical to drive effective and efficient implementation of e-commerce reforms. UNCTAD has consistently supported the development of coordination structures and capacities to monitor policy recommendations and measures featured in assessments, strategies and policies. Those efforts aim to build inclusive and results-driven governance models adapted to each country and region. UNCTAD works closely with eTrade focal points to ensure clear leadership within Governments.

[24] The courses are organized in collaboration with digital trade experts from various international organizations, including WTO, the United Nations Commission on International Trade Law, UNCTAD, the Economic and Social Commission for Asia and the Pacific and the Commonwealth.

[25] The Trade Policy Training Centre in Africa organized a series of awareness-raising workshops in Malawi in 2024, focusing on the importance of digital trade in the AfCFTA context and implications for various sectors. The workshops were built upon more advanced trade negotiation training focusing on negotiations in the annexes of the Digital Trade Protocol and the WTO Joint Statement Initiative on E-commerce.

[26] See https://au-afcfta.org/2025/05/afcfta-digital-trade-forum-2025-concludes-with-strong-commitments-to-implementation-and-inclusion.

Typically, mid- to senior-level officials within lead ministries (usually trade, less frequently ICT or digital affairs or foreign affairs) help drive e-commerce policymaking. Independently of the institutional leadership, having well-functioning interministerial coordination is important. Core elements of such governance model include:

- A lead agency with a dedicated unit to coordinate reforms (acting as an implementation unit and secretariat for an interministerial technical committee).
- An interministerial committee, acting as coordination body in charge of supervising implementation, advising policy development and reporting to high-level government leadership.
- Inclusive stakeholder engagement, involving public and private sectors and other stakeholders collaborating through the interministerial committee, either through permanent membership or participation by invitation.

The examples below come from Jordan, Kenya, Mauritania, Peru, Rwanda, Samoa and Vanuatu, all of which have set up national e-commerce committees with clear roles and coordination structures:

- As recommended in its e-commerce strategy, in 2023, Jordan established an e-commerce national committee, chaired by the Secretary-General of the Ministry of Industry, Trade and Supply. It includes representatives from various public and private sector institutions and works through technical groups to support e-commerce policy implementation, fundraising, coordination with development partners, as well as public and private sector entities. The committee convenes twice a year (or at the Chair's request) to report on the strategy's implementation, while technical groups meet quarterly to track progress. An e-commerce unit within the Ministry's Trade Directorate serves as the committee's secretariat, holding monthly meetings to coordinate and monitor e-commerce initiatives carried out by public and private sector institutions, as well as civil society organizations.
- In Kenya, in December 2023, UNCTAD organized a workshop to support a newly formed National E-commerce Strategy implementation committee, comprising 27 institutions from the public and private sector. Since then, GIZ has continued to provide operational support, which has resulted in the organization of the committee's inaugural meeting and subsequent planning and review meetings in 2024. Chaired by the Permanent Secretary for Trade and the Permanent Secretary for ICT, the committee is coordinated by the Department for Trade, acting as a full-time secretariat in charge of resource mobilization, including coordination of project proposals, organization of meetings and preparation of documentation.
- In Mauritania, a multi-stakeholder committee led by the Ministry of Digital Transformation, Innovation and Modernization of the Administration, comprising the Ministry of Commerce, other ministries, the private sector, and civil society and consumer organizations, has been set up to follow up on eT Ready recommendations, including the development of a national e-commerce strategy, which started in early 2025. Both the eT Ready and the e-commerce strategy benefited from UNCTAD and GIZ support under the Union for the Mediterranean Hub for Jobs, Trade and Investment project and the Promotion of digital transformation (DIGITAL-Y) project, respectively.
- Peru is in the process of transforming the National Technical Committee for E-commerce, which was temporarily constituted in 2022 to guide eT Ready preparations, into a committee of a permanent nature.[27]

[27] As at June 2025, of the 28 entities invited to participate in the permanent committee, 25 had confirmed their participation through an official document and 3 had yet to do so. Once all entities confirm their participation, the resolution creating the permanent committee will be issued.

- In Rwanda, the Ministry of Trade and Industry accommodates two e-commerce positions to oversee digital trade issues. The implementation of the e-commerce agenda is coordinated through an e-commerce technical working group, formed by key government institutions with e-commerce expertise.
- In Samoa, the National E-commerce Committee oversees the implementation of the E-commerce Strategy launched in 2022. Chaired by the Chief Executive Officer of the Ministry of Commerce, Industry and Labour and co-chaired by the Chief Executive Officer of the Ministry of Foreign Affairs and Trade, it includes seven other key ministries and organizations; it held its first meeting in September 2024.
- In Vanuatu, a full-time officer was appointed in September 2024 to oversee and monitor the implementation of the National E-commerce Strategy. The National E-commerce Committee, led by the Ministry of Tourism, Trade, Commerce and Ni-Vanuatu Businesses, meets three times a year to guide and monitor progress in coordination with the National Trade Development Committee leading the trade development agenda (see annex I).

Without stronger institutional capacity, sustained investment and inter-agency cooperation, governance mechanisms for e-commerce reforms remain fragile and struggle to meet expectations.

While political commitment is an essential first step, without stronger institutional capacity, sustained investment and inter-agency cooperation, governance mechanisms for e-commerce reforms remain fragile and struggle to meet expectations. While progress is being made across countries, persistent challenges, including limited staff, high staff turnover, overlapping responsibilities and competing priorities, continue to undermine the transformative potential of reform structures. The following examples illustrate both the progress made and various institutional challenges:

- In 2022, the Ministry of Trade and Industry of Côte d'Ivoire established an electronic commerce department, reflecting a clear commitment to promote e-commerce. However, operational effectiveness is constrained by the limited availability of staff within the Ministry who can dedicate the necessary time to support the e-commerce reform process and the budget allocated to the unit (approximately $50,000 annually).
- In Bangladesh, a digital commerce authority act was drafted in 2023 but is yet to be enacted. The proposed authority aims to enhance the autonomy and mandate of the Central Digital Commerce Cell under the Ministry of Commerce, including conducting regulatory oversight and addressing consumer protection complaints. However, the Cell operates with limited capacity to oversee digital trade issues and lead inter-agency coordination across ministries, regulators and private sector actors. The delay in the act's approval underscores the challenge of translating legislative processes into institutional impact without sufficient technical and operational reinforcement.
- Nepal demonstrates a proactive approach with the Ministry of Industry, Commerce and Supplies coordinating the implementation of the 2019 national e-commerce strategy through regular consultation meetings. However, many of the stakeholders involved hold multiple roles, which limits their availability and sustained engagement, highlighting the need for dedicated resources to effectively support cross-sectoral collaboration.
- In Solomon Islands, the establishment of the E-commerce Implementation Unit, created under the Ministry of Commerce, Industry, Labour and Immigration in 2024, and its operationalization in 2025, after securing the necessary budget and recruiting staff, reflects a promising structural development. However, the time required to get the Unit up and running points to the challenges

faced in institutionalizing new reform mechanisms.

- Tonga has made progress by assigning the responsibility for the implementation and monitoring of the national e-commerce strategy to a facilitation unit within the Ministry of Trade and Economic Development. However, persistent human resource limitations, exacerbated by high staff turnover, have slowed momentum. Despite plans to expand the unit, currently run by one person, onboarding more staff will require substantial training. Tonga also has the National E-commerce Committee, but it is confronted with conflicting priorities and members' availability in holding regular meetings.
- In Tuvalu, the Department of Trade has recently established a new structure that includes a director, three trade officers and an administrative and finance officer. While the National E-commerce Committee was established in 2022, its operationalization suffered from high turnover of staff from several departments and insufficient institutional memory, with no structured handover in place.

Monitoring progress of e-commerce reforms is gaining importance; sophisticated tracking tools would make the process more efficient. While many countries have set up coordination structures, these are often underused due to challenges in bringing key stakeholders and limited resources for proper monitoring and evaluation. Few countries have dedicated monitoring and evaluation officers, and structured systems are rare. However, a few countries are leading by example:

- The Ministry of Commerce of Cambodia has produced regular annual reports on the e-commerce landscape since 2020, offering insights into policies, regulations and market trends for both policymakers and the private sector.[28]
- The National Technical Committee for E-commerce in Peru reported, in November 2024, that of the 60 eT Ready recommendations, 44 had been addressed (representing a 73 per cent implementation rate).
- In its evaluation of the implementation of the 2022–2023 action plan, the Ministry of Trade and Export Development of Tunisia noted that 42 per cent of the measures had been implemented, 35 per cent were in progress and 23 per cent had not started. A second action plan, for 2024–2025, has been prepared to capitalize on achievements and reprioritize work.
- The National E-commerce Committee of Vanuatu noted, in April 2025, that 25 per cent of the strategy's recommendations had been fully implemented, while 40 per cent were under way, including those on digital literacy, MSME support and e-payment systems, and 35 per cent still required urgent action.

Efforts are also under way at regional levels:

- In the EAC region, national structures are increasingly interconnected through the EAC E-commerce Engagement Platform. A monitoring and evaluation framework was adopted in November 2024 and finalized in May 2025, including monitoring tools (based on spreadsheets) to facilitate data collection and reporting.[29]

[28] In the latest report (2024), the Ministry indicated that greater integration in ASEAN represents a major opportunity for Cambodia to further integrate itself into regional and global digital markets, especially in view of the expected benefits that would result from the implementation of the Digital Economy Framework Agreement. See https://api.techostartup.center/media/files/PROFITENCE_2024_E-commerce_Report_2.pdf.

[29] The outcome-level tool focuses on 23 key performance indicators, while the process-level tool focuses on tracking progress on implementing the 60 measures outlined in the regional strategy. Both tools are part of the digital East African Monitoring System.

- In the ECOWAS region, progress is recorded through interactions with member States by its Trade Directorate, which feeds into the overall macro-level monitoring of different ECOWAS programmes.
- The PIF secretariat uses the Pacific E-commerce Portal as both a knowledge hub and a monitoring and evaluation platform. Annual monitoring reports are produced, featuring implementation metrics based on a weighting system that considers the contribution of each relevant project and programme implemented in the region towards the delivery of targets of the Regional E-commerce Strategy. In the 2024 report, the secretariat indicated that 65 per cent of the Strategy's measures were in progress, with an overall implementation rate 30.46 per cent and partners' support amounting to approximately $152.9 million.

Going forward, countries and regions should improve monitoring using digital solutions to simplify reporting and enhance transparency. The eTrade Reform Tracker, developed in cooperation with the eTrade focal points from the Implementation Support Mechanism partner countries, is currently being rolled out in several countries and is aimed at supporting more effective reform tracking and coordination (box 2).

Box 2
Roll-out of the eTrade Reform Tracker: preliminary takeaways and future perspectives

The Tracker provides a collaborative and user-friendly platform where users can assign tasks, track progress and report on results in real time. It also captures the involvement of development partners, helping countries better monitor mobilization efforts. Documents such as meeting minutes, workplans and reports can be uploaded and stored directly in the system, making information-sharing more efficient and transparent. Accurate and timely data entry through the Tracker is expected to support informed decision-making and simplify reporting.

The Tracker is offered on a demand-driven basis and is governed by a licence agreement. An indicative roll-out road map serves as a guide for partner countries to mobilize key stakeholders and for UNCTAD to tailor roll-out strategies to national context. Development partners can contribute to the Tracker roll-out efforts, by offering assistance for training sessions and coordination support or technical assistance.

One year after its official launch,[a] the Tracker has gained traction. As at July 2025, the following countries and regions had requested to use the Tracker or expressed a clear interest: Fiji, Ghana, Jordan, Kenya, Mauritania, Peru, Samoa, Solomon Islands, Trinidad and Tobago, Zimbabwe and the ECOWAS Commission. Roll-out activities are ongoing and training sessions are under way in most of those countries and regions. Early feedback has been positive with stakeholders appreciating the intuitive design of the tool and the training support provided by UNCTAD. However, partner countries have also indicated that training conducted online is less effective and risks overstretching their limited capacities. Therefore, they recommend in-person training sessions and regular on-site follow-up for sustained engagement and impact. Capacity-building activities to improve coordination among lead implementing agencies and to help them to prioritize actions, together with a more active involvement of the private sector and other relevant stakeholders, is also needed.

In Fiji and Samoa, UNCTAD has provided short-term support by making available a monitoring and evaluation consultant to the lead ministry. The consultants play a key role in facilitating the implementation of their national e-commerce strategies through effective use of the Tracker. By working closely with focal points from various implementing agencies and lead ministries, the consultants will build institutional capacity to manage, update and report through the Tracker.

That support will help strengthen coordination across government and ensure the long-term, sustainable use of the tool, thereby enabling evidence-based decision-making to advance the digital economy.

In Solomon Islands, the lead ministry has a monitoring and evaluation officer within its implementation unit, who benefits from UNCTAD training and advisory support, empowering the unit in the daily use of the Tracker. However, as those interventions are intended to be catalytic and time-bound, it is essential that countries progressively allocate their own resources, both financial and human, to institutionalize the use of such tools. Doing so will ensure sustainable implementation and national ownership of e-commerce reforms over time.

In 2025, training sessions were organized, among others, in:

Solomon Islands

Trinidad and Tobago

Zimbabwe

Source: UNCTAD.
[a] It was officially presented in May 2024 at the eTrade capacity-building workshop organized in conjunction with the seventh session of the Intergovernmental Group of Experts on E-commerce and the Digital Economy (see sect. A above).

D. Strengthening evidence-based e-commerce policymaking

Countries are making slow progress in establishing statistics on e-commerce and digital trade due to significant challenges in data collection. Key issues include the lack of capacities faced by national statistical offices and the inconsistent use of definitions, standardized methodologies and appropriate tools, which hinders the ability to monitor progress and support evidence-based policymaking. One major challenge is the divergence from internationally agreed definitions. While the OECD definition of e-commerce (2009) is widely recognized and followed by UNCTAD (2021),[30] some countries have opted to adopt their own definitions, which diverge from this standard. Others have chosen to expand on the OECD definition and include types of transactions that better reflect the digital commerce landscape in developing countries, such as purchases made through manually typed messages sent using social networks or messaging applications. Those forms of transactions are excluded from the OECD definition but are a growing reality in many developing economies.

Moreover, a significant portion of economic activity in those countries occurs within the informal sector. Sales through messaging platforms and other informal digital channels, referred to as "social commerce" or "mobile commerce", are increasingly used by individuals and households to engage in online selling. As a result, business statistics may not adequately capture the

Lack of capacities faced by national statistical offices, inconsistent use of definitions and inadequate methodologies and tools are hindering the ability to monitor progress and support evidence-based policymaking.

[30] See annex II for the definitions of e-commerce and digital trade.

true scale and volume of digital activity (box 3). Without using harmonized definitions of e-commerce, standardized methods and adequate tools, it is difficult to track progress or inform policymaking effectively.

Box 3
Measuring e-commerce: bridging gaps through increased cooperation and capacity-building

Robust and internationally comparable statistics on the value of e-commerce sales are not widely available. In their absence, various indicators offering partial insights are relied upon, including e-commerce uptake as captured in business and household surveys, statistics on online retail sales, data on remote payments or parcel post volumes (such as those compiled by the Universal Postal Union (UPU)), and analysis produced by business associations or market intelligence firms. Such indicators, if available at all, offer limited possibilities for comparability across countries.

International cooperation is central to harmonize efforts made at the national level, in cooperation with regional organizations and technical agencies. Since 2023, UNCTAD has convened a task group on measuring e-commerce value, which provides a forum for experts with hands-on experience of developing e-commerce statistics to engage in detailed technical discussions. The task group is working actively, through quarterly meetings and an online collaboration platform, to develop international statistical guidelines and recommendations on measuring e-commerce value. Chaired by Thailand, the group benefits from the participation of experts from more than 25 developed and developing economies, as well as relevant international organizations, including OECD and WTO. Those guidelines and recommendations will lay a firm foundation for capacity-building and technical assistance on measuring e-commerce value. Such efforts will complement and build upon previous initiatives, notably the International Monetary Fund, OECD, UNCTAD and WTO capacity-building on measuring digital trade.

Source: UNCTAD.

During the review, some countries indicated that they were developing their own e-commerce definitions, such as Rwanda, or establishing their own mechanisms to overcome data gaps and better capture market trends and certain data on e-commerce. For example:

- Peru is developing a project entitled "Satellite Account for the Digital Economy and E-commerce" to track e-commerce transactions and calculate the digital economy's contribution to the economy.
- Rwanda, in line with its National E-commerce Strategy, developed an Action Plan outlining the required steps to have a comprehensive data collection mechanism that starts from the definition of e-commerce in the Rwandan context. The Ministry of Trade and Industry also established an e-commerce data collection and reporting tool and is now in the process of integrating it with domestic e-commerce platforms, to capture instant data on e-commerce transactions.[31]
- In Togo, the Ministry of the Digital Economy and Digital Transformation is setting up a national digital observatory to collect and monitor data on digitalization projects.

[31] See https://dcrt.minicom.gov.rw/dcrt (last access August 2025).

- In Tunisia, the annual E-commerce Barometer, developed through public-private collaboration, measures and analyses online consumer trends and behaviours. The 2024 edition highlighted stability in online purchasing trends,with changing consumer preferences and behaviours.[32]

Other countries in the present review, including Côte d'Ivoire, Nepal, Senegal and Togo, have expressed interest in building or strengthening market data analytics systems and digital observatories for better data-informed policymaking. As developing countries are looking at ways to establish data-driven systems in support of their policymaking, strengthening the capacities of public administrations in building their statistical capacities will be critical to ensure countries can benefit from the growth of the digital economy.

32 The Barometer aims to fill the gaps in official statistics by providing a comprehensive picture of the Tunisian e-commerce market, focusing specifically on consumer demand. It tracks key e-commerce metrics, such as the penetration rate of e-commerce, the behaviour of online shoppers (age, frequency, types of products purchased, payment methods etc.), the motivations and obstacles to online purchases, as well as purchase intentions and consumer profiles. It was revealed in the fifth survey that the value of the average basket was higher, there had been a shift towards mobile/social e-commerce and cash-on-delivery and there had been growth in the use of pick-up points. The results also highlighted, as predominant criteria for making online purchases, the clarity of the website, the attractiveness of the prices, the possibility of returning the product and short delivery times. See https://www.tunisienumerique.com/exclusif-les-premiers-resultats-et-apprentissages-de-la-vague-5-du-barometre-du-commerce-electronique-en-tunisie (in French).

Chapter II

Main developments in national and regional e-commerce ecosystems

In recent years, the rapid advancement of digital technologies has created significant opportunities and challenges for developing countries, including least developed countries. Although global Internet access has steadily increased, substantial connectivity gaps persist, especially in underserved, rural and remote areas. Bridging that divide is critical to unlocking the full potential of the digital economy. Beyond expanding connectivity, strengthening digital services and infrastructure, including logistics for e-commerce related to goods, and establishing supportive regulatory frameworks are essential to building more inclusive and resilient digital ecosystems. Countries are also prioritizing the development of digital skills and entrepreneurship. Cultivating a workforce proficient in essential digital competencies and improving access to finance for digital start-ups are vital to fostering innovation and competitiveness. In the following sections of the review, key opportunities, challenges and priorities reported by partner countries as part of their efforts to advance sustainable and inclusive digital transformation are highlighted.

A. Improving Internet connectivity and digital services

Developing countries, particularly least developed countries, have increased investments in ICT to improve infrastructure resilience. Those efforts have helped expand connectivity in underserved areas. As of 2024, 68 per cent of the global population had Internet access, reflecting a 4.6 per cent increase from the previous year (ITU, 2024). Nevertheless, an estimated 2.6 billion people were not using the Internet, with the vast majority living in developing countries. The challenge is particularly pronounced in least developed countries and landlocked developing countries, in which Internet penetration stands at just 35 and 39 per cent, respectively (figure III).

According to the International Telecommunication Union (ITU), the urban-rural Internet usage gap has also been stuck at a ratio of approximately 1.7 over the past four years. In 2024, 83 per cent of the urban population was online, compared with just 43 per cent of the rural population. Those disparities are largely due to infrastructure deficits, high connectivity costs and limited digital literacy. Bridging the gaps requires targeted investments, particularly in last-mile connectivity solutions, including fibre-optic deployment, and alternative technologies, such as satellite and community networks. Such investments would be more effective if guided by an "inclusive by design" approach that addresses the needs of marginalized and less digitally connected or skilled communities from the outset. Improved access to Internet would pave the way for digital inclusion, facilitate cloud-based applications, enable secure online transactions and empower businesses, especially MSMEs, and consumers to engage more effectively in global markets. Meeting those challenges is costly. Estimates suggest that approximately $418 billion are required to achieve universal connectivity by 2030 – an essential step towards realizing Sustainable Development Goal 9 and enabling inclusive digital transformation (Oughton, Amaglobeli and Moszoro, 2023).[33]

As of 2024, 68 per cent of the global population had Internet access – yet 2.6 billion people remained offline, most of whom were in developing countries.

Achieving universal connectivity by 2030 – a critical step towards inclusive digital transformation – will require an estimated $418 billion in investment.

[33] This estimate is based on global investment needs to achieve universal broadband connectivity by 2030, as highlighted by ITU, UNESCO and the Broadband Commission for Sustainable Development (2023). It reflects the costs of connecting approximately 2.6 billion unconnected people, primarily in low- and middle-income countries.

Figure 3
Percentage of individuals using the Internet (2019 and 2024)

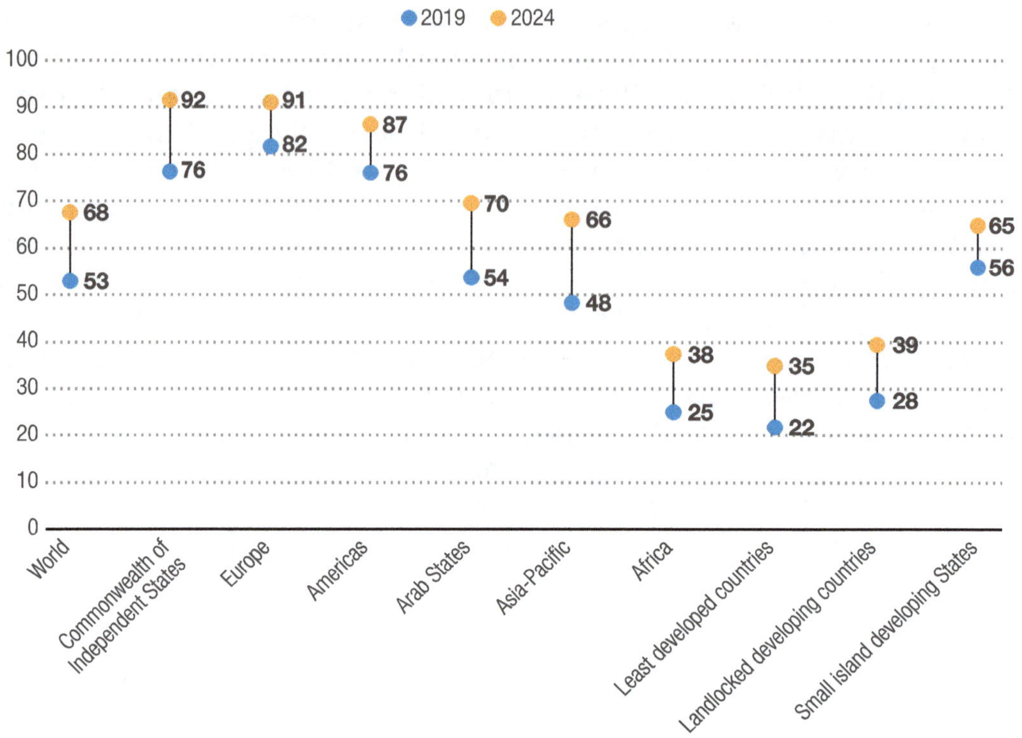

Source: ITU (2024).

Countries reviewed continue to implement large-scale ICT infrastructure projects to expand broadband access, reduce connectivity costs and support inclusive digital growth. Those efforts aim to bridge the digital divide, boost innovation and enable broad-based economic and social development.

In Nepal, broadband penetration has seen steady progress since the introduction of the 4G mobile network in 2017. Mobile coverage had reached 102 subscriptions for every 100 people as at October 2024, with data consumption rising, particularly among the youth. Rural areas, however, still face limited coverage. To address that, the Nepal Telecommunications Authority envisages implementing broadband-friendly policies and incentivizing service providers to expand their networks. Increasing subsidies to the operators for 4G expansion through the Rural Telecommunications Development Fund would also help to bridge the digital divide.

Malawi recently embarked on the ambitious Digital Malawi Acceleration Project, a $150 million initiative to expand Internet access and enhance digital services, building on the earlier Digital Foundations project.[34] By 2030, the project is aimed at installing 2,000 km of fibre-optic cables and improving connectivity for 2,500 institutions, including 2,000 schools and 500 government offices. The project is designed to improve Internet infrastructure, with new cables, communication towers, satellite technologies, village Wi-Fi centres, Internet exchange points and data centres – marking a major step in leveraging digital technology for national growth and public service delivery.

Côte d'Ivoire has also taken major steps to

[34] Led by the Ministry of Information and Digitalization through the Public Private Partnership Commission and funded by the World Bank, the Digital Foundations project is aimed at increasing access to affordable, high-quality Internet services for Government, businesses and citizens and improving the Government's capacity to deliver digital public services. See https://www.pppc.mw/projects/digital-foundations-project.

expand its fibre-optic network, extending coverage to rural and peri-urban areas. As at March 2024, the country had 30,240 km of fibre-optic infrastructure, including 24,600 km operated by the private sector and 5,640 km managed by the State-led network. That network currently covers 8,080 localities out of a planned 8,518, achieving a 94.86 per cent coverage rate. The Government is accelerating the deployment of 4G networks across the country, including in rural areas, while laying the groundwork for 5G roll-out.

At the regional level, EAC is investing to expand connectivity and lower Internet and communication costs through regional collaboration. In 2024, Burundi and the United Republic of Tanzania joined the EAC/GIZ One Network Area initiative, harmonizing roaming and traffic exchange to promote regional trade.[35] In the same year, the Eastern Africa Regional Digital Integration Project was launched by EAC and the Intergovernmental Authority on Development with World Bank support, to bridge infrastructure gaps, reduce end-user costs and improve access to digital services, particularly in underserved rural areas. In the Pacific Island States, expanding Internet connectivity is critical due to their unique geographic isolation and vulnerability to natural disasters.

In the Pacific, Tonga is deploying a second submarine cable network and strengthening the existing link. Meanwhile Tuvalu announced in December 2024 the successful landing of the country's first submarine cable, marking a major leap forward for connectivity and digital inclusion.[36]

Submarine cables are the backbone of Pacific connectivity but remain prone to damage from natural disasters, leading to frequent and costly outages (UNCTAD, 2025d). For example, Tonga has experienced repeated disruptions, with an 80 per cent likelihood of similar incidents recurring. For many small island nations, the reliance on a single cable makes the risk of prolonged Internet blackouts especially high, particularly given the challenges of maintaining and repairing these systems in remote locations. At the same time, advances in cable technology are turning this infrastructure into a tool not just for communication, but also for resilience. New-generation cables, such as SMART TamTam, set to connect New Caledonia and Vanuatu, integrate seismic and environmental sensors capable of detecting earthquakes, tsunamis and other natural events in real time, supporting early warning systems while acting as a backup for the existing ICN1 cable that links Vanuatu to Fiji. That redundancy helps mitigate the impact of potential disruptions.[37] In parallel, the ITU-supported SMART Island Project is enhancing connectivity and digital skills in countries such as Vanuatu, Fiji and Papua New Guinea. To date, it has reached more than 5,000 beneficiaries, contributing to more resilient and inclusive digital ecosystems across the region.

Satellite technology is increasingly seen as an alternative solution to traditional land-sea Internet connectivity networks, especially for remote and underserved areas in which laying cables is challenging. While that technology offers rapid deployment and wider coverage, satellite Internet is not always more cost-effective than fibre-optic networks due to higher equipment costs, subscription fees and potential limitations in speed and latency. Nonetheless, its portability and flexibility make it a crucial complement to submarine cables, helping to bridge connectivity gaps where traditional infrastructure is impractical. For the Pacific Islands, where mobile broadband is still unaffordable for many, a hybrid model – combining submarine cables and satellite networks – could ensure more inclusive and reliable Internet

[35] Kenya, Rwanda, South Sudan and Uganda were already members of the initiative.

[36] The Tuvalu Vaka Cable project is developed by Tuvalu Telecommunications Corporation, in collaboration with Google, as part of its Central Pacific Connect Initiative.

[37] The project is funded by France and will be implemented by the Government of Vanuatu and the Post and Telecommunications Office of New Caledonia.

access (UNCTAD, 2025d). For example, "Pocket Internet" devices, such as the Starlink Mini, introduced recently in Fiji, provide Internet speeds of up to 150 Mbps for a relatively affordable price. Choosing between submarine fibre-optic cables and alternative satellite solutions must balance investment priorities against the unique challenges of scattered populations and the pressing need for reliable and affordable Internet access. For instance, Starlink's service fees of about $99 a month in Fiji, Kiribati and Vanuatu are still not much lower than submarine cable-based broadband.

African countries are also increasingly adopting satellite technology to provide Internet access, especially to remote communities. To date, 18 countries have signed partnership agreements with Space-X Starlink, including Ghana, Kenya, the Niger and Zambia.[38] Despite its smaller subscriber base compared with established broadband providers, Starlink is the fastest growing Internet service provider in Kenya, with a 90 per cent growth rate. Since July 2023, its network of thousands of small satellites extends high-speed coverage to remote areas lacking traditional infrastructure, offering, for example, users in the Niger speeds of up to 200 Mbps for approximately $40 a month. Other satellite providers, such as OneWeb and newcomer Q-KON, are also strengthening their foothold in Africa, focusing on affordable, hybrid satellite and terrestrial models to connect underserved rural areas in West and East Africa through partnerships with local Governments and telecommunications operators. That approach is designed to provide reliable Internet access with competitive pricing, further diversifying the continent's satellite broadband ecosystem and expanding options for consumers and businesses alike.

Beyond connectivity, affordability continues to be a critical barrier to digital inclusion. While global mobile broadband prices dropped slightly in 2024 to 1.1 per cent of gross national income per capita, people in least developed countries still allocate a disproportionately large proportion of their budget to access the Internet (ITU, 2024). The affordability gap has widened, with African mobile Internet costs 14 times higher than in Europe, up from 12 times in 2023 (figure 4).

Increased connectivity has been a major catalyst for the growth of digital services in developing regions, unlocking access to e-commerce, fintech, e-government and digital platforms. As mobile broadband penetration has expanded, millions of people in Africa, Asia and Latin America have gained access to digital tools that were previously out of reach. In sub-Saharan Africa, where 4G coverage reached 92 per cent in 2024, digital services, particularly mobile money services, have revolutionized financial transactions, spurred cross-border trade and advanced financial inclusion (see sect. C below). Integrated mobile-based platforms are also revolutionizing key sectors, such as agriculture and healthcare. In Kenya, for example, the DigiFarm platform helps smallholder farmers to connect with markets and receive payments. In the Pacific region, the Maua e-commerce platform, introduced in Samoa in 2018, has recently scaled up operations in Vanuatu, empowering businesses, especially in remote areas, to expand their reach and strengthen local economies.

At the same time, digitalization within Governments – particularly through public procurement and service delivery systems – has become a strategic entry point for building institutional capabilities. By adopting digital tools internally, Governments not only enhance service delivery but also acquire critical skills and infrastructure that can support a broader, more inclusive digital transition. That institutional learning can reinforce trust in digital systems, foster interoperability and drive demand for locally relevant digital services and innovation.

[38] See https://www.starlink.com/map.

Figure 4
Data-only mobile broadband basket prices as a percentage of gross national income per capita (2023 and 2024)

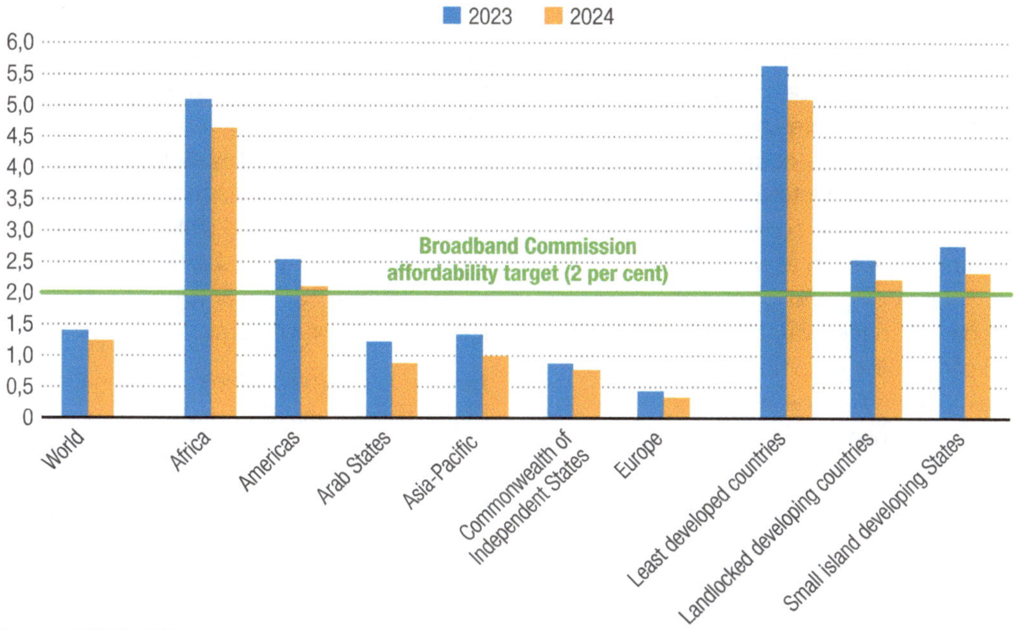

Source: ITU (2024).
Note: prices refer to the cheapest mobile broadband plan providing at least 2 GB of monthly data using at least 3G technology.

Nevertheless, persistent challenges, such as unstable Internet connectivity, high data costs and digital literacy gaps, remain barriers to fully leveraging those services. Addressing those issues through increased infrastructure investment, supportive policy reforms and digital skills developments will be critical to ensure that digital transformation is inclusive and far-reaching. In parallel, improved connectivity has also accelerated the development of digital identity systems, which are increasingly vital for accessing a wide range of services, from banking to government programmes, particularly in remote areas underserved by traditional systems. In Africa, countries such as Ghana and Kenya are strengthening their existing digital identity systems to prevent fraud and enhance public service delivery. In Malawi, the Digital Malawi Acceleration Project includes the establishment of secure and interoperable data platforms, a government data exchange system and digital identities to enable safe and reliable access to online services such as banking. The Single Digital Identification System in Rwanda, launched in 2023, now covers more than 90 per cent of the population, enabling seamless access to government services, banking and mobile connectivity. Zambia is also advancing digital identity as part of its 2024 partnership with the World Bank Identification for Development Initiative, aimed at modernizing digital public infrastructure as a foundation for a new digital identification system. Those national efforts are aligned with the continental blueprint of the Smart Africa Trust Alliance and the African Union Interoperability Framework for Digital ID by adopting common standards, mutual-recognition mechanisms and governance structures that enable cross-border digital identity use. The coordinated approach of Smart Africa supports interoperable and trusted digital public infrastructure across its members.[39]

Unstable Internet connectivity, high data costs and digital literacy gaps remain major barriers to fully leveraging digital services.

[39] See https://smartafrica.org/sas-project/digital-identity-for-africa.

B. Facilitating e-commerce logistics and digital trade

Improving last-mile delivery remains a key driver for reforms aimed at developing logistics infrastructure and services tailored to the demands of e-commerce related to goods. In today's fast-paced e-commerce landscape, meeting core customer expectations – such as rapid delivery, real-time tracking and logistical flexibility – depends on the availability of efficient and competitive e-commerce logistics infrastructure. As a result, countries are increasingly investing in the modernization of their logistics systems by leveraging digital technologies, such as mobile applications, GPS-based address mapping, AI and solutions based on the Internet of things. Those tools enhance inventory management, order fulfilment and shipment tracking, contributing to more agile and resilient supply chains. At the same time, an increasing number of countries leverage their existing network of post offices, especially in remote districts, and convert them into multi-channel service delivery one-stop shops for MSMEs, artisans and women entrepreneurs.

Three in four shippers now prioritize environmentally responsible logistics when exporting to high-income countries.

In Kenya, GoBEBA, a technology-driven logistics start-up, is transforming the distribution of bulky essentials by deploying a distributed network of micro-fulfilment hubs in underserved areas. The company integrates automation, AI and robotics to overcome infrastructure constraints, enabling faster and more reliable urban deliveries. The platform aims to expand beyond Kenya to several African cities, tapping into unmet demand in rapidly urbanizing areas. In Nepal, in addition to reforms that have decentralized the postal codes to the local (ward) level, expanded the reach of the Nepal Postal Office and implemented a tracking and tracing system, plans are under way to establish rural logistics hubs by 2025 to strengthen last-mile delivery and lower distribution costs. Meanwhile, Vanuatu is modernizing its delivery infrastructure through the introduction of a standardized national addressing system and postal codes, reducing reliance on the State-run postal service and enhancing service reliability. Similarly, Solomon Islands has also emphasized plans to strengthen e-commerce distribution and delivery services by establishing pick-up and drop-off points and improving last-mile solutions in rural areas.

Beyond last-mile solutions, strong national and regional transport networks form the backbone of effective e-commerce logistics. Without well-functioning road, rail, air and port systems, even the most advanced digital platforms cannot ensure timely delivery or scale operations efficiently. Countries such as Bangladesh are investing in multimodal transport corridors to support rising volumes of e-commerce deliveries.

Sustainability is also emerging as a core principle of modern logistics systems. Investment in green logistics, including low-emission transport and energy-efficient warehousing, is gaining momentum globally. Currently, approximately 75 per cent of shippers prioritize environmentally responsible logistics options when exporting to high-income countries (World Bank, 2023). The postal sector advances sustainability and e-commerce through streamlined last-mile delivery and data-driven innovation. Leveraging the Online Solution for Carbon Analysis and Reporting platform of UPU, postal operators in many countries can now monitor emissions, analyse logistics data and improve service quality, while supporting climate action.

In Africa, Rwanda is emerging as a regional leader in that area. With the 2024 launch of the Kigali Logistics Platform Connect Project, the Government aims to integrate multimodal transport systems, improve connections to the Bugesera Industrial Park and offer dedicated e-commerce services. Environmental protection, road safety and trade facilitation are emphasized in the project, as a way to foster a greener and more inclusive trade ecosystem. That growing focus on sustainable logistics complements broader efforts to reduce the environmental footprint of the digital economy – including the energy consumption of ICT infrastructure and the responsible sourcing of materials (box 4).

Countries and regions have progressed at a sustained pace in implementing trade facilitation reforms, however, cross-border paperless trade remains a major bottleneck. The global trade facilitation implementation rate rose to 70 per cent in 2025, up from 66 per cent in 2023, with only a modest increase in paperless trade adoption (figure 5).[40] However, estimates show that digital trade facilitation reforms could reduce overall trade costs by up to 14 per cent (United Nations, 2023).

Digital trade facilitation reforms could cut global trade costs by up to 14 per cent.

Box 4
Environmental aspects of e-commerce and the digital economy

The rapid expansion of e-commerce and the broader digital economy has profound environmental implications, especially in transport, energy consumption and resource use. Transport associated with e-commerce, including last-mile delivery, return logistics and the increasing volume of shipments, is responsible for nearly 7 per cent of global greenhouse gas emissions, driven largely by road freight vehicles. As online shopping and digital services scale up, the energy demand of supporting ICT infrastructure, such as data centres, networks and user devices, continues to rise steeply. Data centres alone consume about 1 per cent of global electricity today, with projections suggesting that could triple by 2030 if left unchecked (UNCTAD, 2024a). Combined with networks and user devices, the overall digital economy energy consumption could reach nearly 10 per cent of global electricity demand within a decade. Moreover, e-commerce's reliance on digital devices and batteries drives demand for critical minerals, such as lithium, cobalt and rare earth elements. Extracting those resources involves environmental challenges, including habitat disruption and pollution, underscoring the urgent need for better recycling and e-waste management to reduce the digital economy's ecological footprint.

In response to those challenges, innovative sustainable initiatives are emerging. Bangladesh plans to develop its first green data centre near Chattogram, through a public-private partnership involving the Bangladesh Telecommunications Company Limited, the Asian Development Bank and the Public-Private Partnership Authority. That advanced facility will be powered entirely by renewable energy and built to international standards for high availability and scalability, providing commercial colocation services to both the public and private sectors while supporting the Telecommunications Company's own data storage needs. The project exemplifies how sustainable digital infrastructure investments can unlock private sector capital and drive innovation, aligning with global efforts to decarbonize the digital economy, and sets a strong example for other developing countries. The initiative reflects a broader trend identified by UNCTAD, where mobilizing green investments and enhancing energy efficiency are critical to balancing the benefits of digital growth with environmental sustainability.

Source: UNCTAD.

Transport linked to e-commerce accounts for nearly 7 per cent of global greenhouse gas emissions.

[40] The trade facilitation implementation rate represents the percentage of trade facilitation measures that a country has implemented. The rate is calculated on the basis of 31 general and digital trade facilitation measures, both binding and non-binding provisions from the WTO Trade Facilitation Agreement, as well as broader digital and sustainable trade practices.

Figure 5
Trade facilitation and paperless trade (2025)
(Percentage)

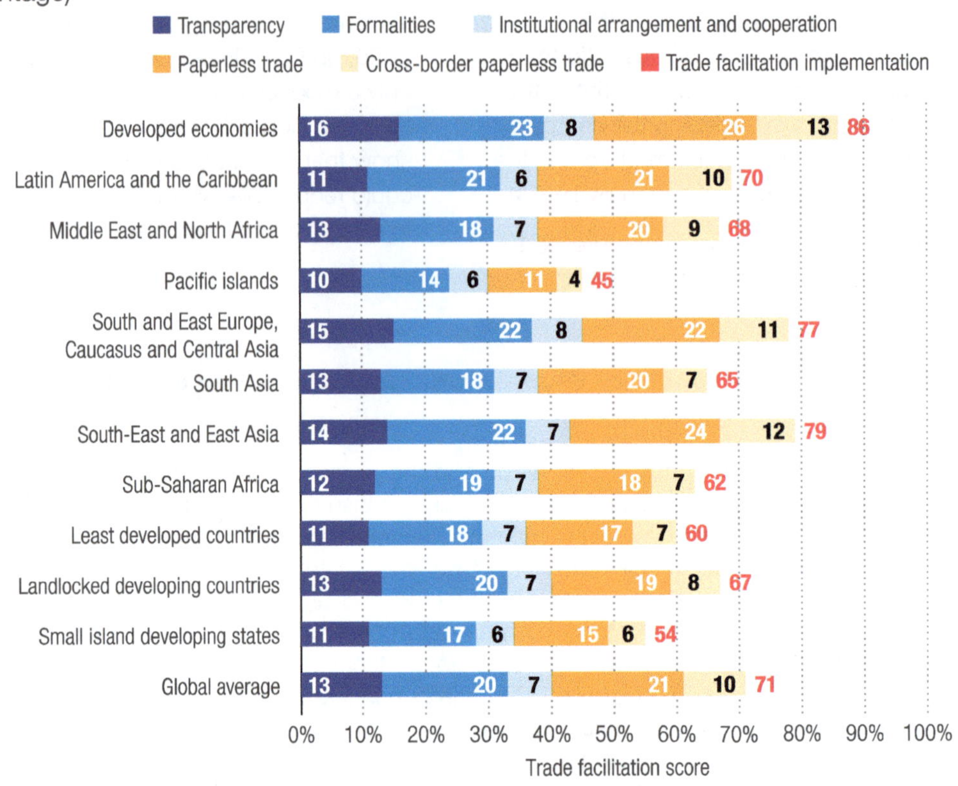

Source: United Nations (2025).

Key enablers of trade facilitation include the adoption of automated customs clearance systems, national single windows, legal and transit reforms supporting electronic transactions and enhanced intergovernmental coordination.

The Government of Mongolia is preparing for a major customs reform in 2025, centred on the launch of a single electronic window to streamline government services related to foreign trade procedures. Supported by the Asian Development Bank and managed by the General Department of Customs, the reform will be rolled out in two phases: first, by developing an integrated electronic system for processing permits, licences and customs clearances; and, second, by deploying a risk management system and the necessary servers and hardware to support the single electronic window. As a party to the Framework Agreement on Facilitation of Cross-border Paperless Trade in Asia and the Pacific, Mongolia has also developed a national action plan to support its implementation and advance trade digitalization.[41] In South Asia, the National Logistics Policy 2024 of Bangladesh sets out a strategic blueprint for efficient and environmentally sustainable logistics. The policy is aimed at establishing logistics hubs, international corridors and economic zones, while modernizing airport and port cargo handling to support export growth and deeper integration into global value chains. Complementing that, the Bangladesh Cross-border Digital Commerce Policy 2024, soon to be finalized, is designed to simplify the import and export of goods between Bangladesh and other countries through digital platforms, align the country's digital commerce framework with global standards and provide small and medium-sized enterprises (SMEs) with simplified export policies, guidelines and financial incentives for e-commerce exports. To bolster those reforms, Bangladesh is also enhancing

[41] The plan was debated and adopted during the second meeting of the National Working Group, held as part of the Digital Trade Week in Mongolia in March 2025 (see chap. I, sect. B).

the Central Logistics Tracking Platform and offering targeted training to logistics providers on cross-border e-commerce.

In Africa, Tunisia is operationalizing SINDA II,[42] an advanced digital customs platform designed to fully automate documentation, integrate risk management protocols and ensure interoperability and traceability across the overall trade ecosystem. The initiative is built upon the country's strong track record in e-governance, following the successful implementation of flagship projects such as the Tunisia e-Procurement System. It also complements the role of Tunisia Trade Net, which functions as the country's national single window for foreign trade formalities. To further boost its e-commerce potential, Tunisia is adopting the Easy Export model of UPU, which simplifies export procedures for MSMEs and strengthens digital trade infrastructure – improving delivery services, fostering entrepreneurship and enabling local businesses to compete globally through better postal-customs coordination.

Zambia, in collaboration with Angola and the Democratic Republic of the Congo, is advancing the Lobito Corridor project to create a strategic transport route to the Angolan coast. The corridor is expected to reduce logistics costs, boost export competitiveness and enhance regional integration.[43] Similarly, in February 2025, the Niger announced plans to develop a dry port in Agadez to support future railway expansion and reduce dependency on coastal ports. The project will serve as a logistics hub for customs processing, quality control and goods storage, facilitating trade with Algeria, Chad and Libya.

To modernize its trade framework and improve the business environment, Togo is carrying out, in the broader context of AfCFTA implementation, several key reforms aligned with regional efforts to harmonize trade facilitation reforms and promote a coherent business environment in West Africa. Since January 2024, ITC has been supporting the Ministry of Trade, Handicrafts and Local Consumption of Togo in developing its Trade Portal, an online platform that provides step-by-step guidance on import and export procedures from the trader's perspective.[44] It currently covers more than 50 procedures and 13 strategic product groups critical to the economy of Togo, with further expansion under way. In parallel, Togo reactivated its Trade Barrier Alert Mechanism in February 2025, enabling businesses to: (a) promptly report challenges in import/export operations to the relevant authorities; (b) provide real-time data to business support institutions on trade obstacles; and (c) help public authorities identify and address trade barriers.

At the regional level, the EAC secretariat launched the Electronic Tariff (E-Tariff) software in 2024, with support from the European Union-World Customs Organization Harmonized System Africa Programme. By offering features such as preferential tariff management, Harmonized System code migration tools and data analytics, the software is designed to enhance efficiency and transparency of customs' operations and revenue collection across EAC partner States. To further improve intra-regional trade, the secretariat also upgraded its Single Customs Territory platform in January 2025. Established in 2014, that centralized system enables real-time data-sharing across the customs and port authorities of member States.[45] By simplifying and expediting the movement of goods, the initiative has already reduced border crossing times by 70 per cent, saving an estimated $63 million annually.[46] It currently integrates

42 See https://www.douane.gov.tn/projet-sinda-2.

43 The project is jointly funded by the African Development Bank, the African Finance Corporation, the European Union and the United States of America.

44 Developed under the ProComp programme (funded by Germany and the European Union and implemented by GIZ), the portal (https://togotrade.gouv.tg) lists required documents, forms, certifications, fees and contact information for relevant border agencies.

45 The platform was launched in 2017 with several upgrades, including those related to maritime trade, managing regional authorized economic opportunities and sharing scanned images for customs transparency.

46 See https://www.trademarkafrica.com/press-release/eac-unveils-single-customs-territory-platform-for-customs-and-port-data-exchange-to-ease-trade.

systems from Burundi, Kenya, Rwanda, Uganda and the United Republic of Tanzania, with plans for further expansion.

Customs systems in the Pacific are also undergoing significant upgrades, with enhanced automation and clearance operations supported by the European Union-UNCTAD Improving Pacific Islands Customs and Trade (IMPACT) project. In 2024, both Fiji and Papua New Guinea signed on to adopt the Automated System for Customs Data (ASYCUDA) blueprint, aiming to implement tailored electronic single window systems aligned with existing national priorities, regional integration and international standards. According to the United Nations (2023), Fiji has implemented 52 per cent of the measures related to global paperless trade under the Agreement on Trade Facilitation, up from 35 per cent in 2015. That progress, driven by the upgrade to ASYCUDA, has led to a two-thirds reduction in customs clearance formalities for both imports and exports (United Nations, 2023). Building on that momentum, Tonga is also seeking support to implement the electronic payment module of ASYCUDA and establish its own national single window, reinforcing the region's broader shift towards more efficient and paperless trade systems.

Despite significant investments in logistics infrastructure and improvements in transit mechanisms, trade flows, particularly cross-border, are increasingly affected by a complex interplay of geopolitical tensions, environmental challenges, rising inflation and the ongoing disruption to global supply chains. The compounded effects of those factors are creating a more volatile and unpredictable environment for businesses and Governments, often leading to delays and higher costs for international trade. The recent imposition of sweeping tariffs by major economies has further complicated the global trade landscape, underscoring the urgent need for increased international cooperation on trade policy and digital commerce to foster resilience and stability in the face of such uncertainties.

C. Developing platforms and seamless integration for digital payments

Global mobile money accounts reached 1.75 billion in 2023, processing $1.4 trillion annually.

In 2024, 40 per cent of adults in sub-Saharan Africa had a mobile money account, up from 27 per cent in 2021.

The accelerated growth of innovative and integrated e-payment systems is transforming the global digital economy, facilitating faster, safer and more efficient transactions. Mobile money has become a transformative force in developing countries, significantly reshaping financial ecosystems and bolstering e-commerce growth. By enabling users to store, send and receive money through mobile devices without traditional bank accounts, those services have extended financial inclusion to previously unbanked populations. As of 2023, there were 1.75 billion registered mobile money accounts worldwide, processing approximately $1.4 trillion annually (GSMA, 2024). In sub-Saharan Africa alone, mobile money contributed an estimated $600 billion to gross domestic product between 2012 and 2022, highlighting its substantial economic impact. Use cases are evolving also as mobile money users shift away from basic transactions to more varied services. International remittances are now one of the fastest growing use cases of mobile money, while merchant payments expanded by 14 per cent, to almost $74 billion in 2023 (ibid.).

Mobile money has also been instrumental in advancing e-commerce in regions with low traditional banking penetration. In 2024, 40 per cent of adults in sub-Saharan Africa had a mobile money account, up from 27 per cent in 2021.[47] Mobile money services, such

[47] World Bank Global Financial Inclusion (Global Findex) Database (2025).

as M-Pesa in Kenya and MTN Mobile Money (MoMo) in Ghana, have contributed to facilitating digital transactions and expanding the customer base for e-commerce. As at December 2024, Côte d'Ivoire had reached more than 26 million mobile money subscribers (with a penetration rate of 82 per cent) across all operators, according to the national regulatory authority.[48]

Nepal has also experienced a significant surge in mobile payments over the past three years, particularly through QR code-based transactions. According to a recent Rastra Bank report, digital payments increased by 43.5 per cent between 2021 and 2024, with transaction values growing by an average of 23.7 per cent. QR code-based payments alone saw an average annual increase of 230 per cent in transaction volume and a 210 per cent year-on-year growth in transaction value. Mobile banking users more than doubled, from 114 million in July 2020 to 265 million by January 2024, with a net preference for QR payments instead of ATM transactions.[49] Despite that steady growth, challenges persist, including a digital divide and insufficient infrastructure in rural areas. Poor mobile connectivity outside Kathmandu has discouraged merchants from adopting digital payments due to concerns about transaction failures. The rise in online scams also underscores the need for increased public awareness and cybersecurity measures.

In the Pacific region, a new cross-border mobile money service was launched in 2023, connecting Vodafone's M-PAiSA and M-Vatu services, paving the way for instant, low-cost international money transfers and e-commerce transactions. That development is part of a broader strategy to interconnect Vodafone's mobile money platforms across the Pacific, including M-Tala in Samoa, E-Moni in the Cook Islands and M-PAiSA in Kiribati, promoting a unified digital payment ecosystem in the region.[50]

Interoperability systems have continued to grow in many countries in response to the growing demand for integrated digital solutions. By streamlining financial flows and improving efficiency, those systems play a pivotal role in reducing costs for businesses and decreasing cash dependency among consumers. They also foster greater transparency, security and financial inclusion, particularly in countries in which access to traditional banking services remains limited. Interoperability – both within countries and among countries – has improved significantly in many developing regions, driven by targeted policy reforms, increasingly integrated mobile money ecosystems and investment in digital financial infrastructure. Key innovations include the establishment of real-time gross settlement (RTGS) systems and automated clearing houses, which enable seamless financial flows across platforms.

Interoperability systems cut costs, boost efficiency and drive financial inclusion in markets with limited banking access.

In Rwanda, the eKash payment system, operated by RSwitch, entered its second phase at the end of 2023, expanding to include all licensed commercial banks and mobile money operators, with plans to integrate microfinance institutions, savings and credit cooperatives, as well as fintech companies. Originally launched in May 2022 to address long-standing market fragmentation in the country's financial ecosystem, the system serves more than 5 million subscribers.

Solomon Islands took a major step forward in August 2024 with the launch of its RTGS, known as the Solomon Islands Automated Transfer System, which significantly enhanced payment efficiency and expanded access to banking services for citizens. With the infrastructure now in place, the Central Bank of Solomon Islands is exploring the integration of a national payment switch, a unified payment interface, and application programming interface-based connections with other payment service providers to increase interoperability and streamline

[48] See https://www.artci.ci/images/stories/pdf/rapport_activite/Rapport_Annuel_-_2024_MAJ_28_04_25.pdf.
[49] See https://www.nrb.org.np/contents/uploads/2025/01/Payment-Oversight-Report-2023-24.pdf.
[50] These initiatives are carried out as part of the Pacific Digital Economy Programme, implemented jointly by UNCTAD, UNCDF and UNDP.

operations. A comparable national digital payment platform was introduced in Vanuatu in 2023 with support from the International Finance Corporation and the World Bank. The system serves as a comprehensive clearing and settlement platform, combining RTGS capabilities for high-value, time-sensitive transactions with an automated clearing house for bulk, low-value payments. It also features a Central Securities Depository, positioning the financial infrastructure of Vanuatu among the most modern in the Pacific region.

In line with the National Financial Inclusion Strategy 2023–2028 of Mauritania, GIMTEL also introduced a national interoperability platform in the country in October 2024. That initiative is aimed at providing citizens with more efficient and rapid access to financial services and forms part of a broader series of reforms carried out by the Central Bank of Mauritania over the past year, including the implementation of an automated clearing system, the launch of an interbank market platform and the activation of oversight mechanisms for payment systems. Collectively, those efforts are paving the way for the establishment of a RTGS system in the country.

More sophisticated digital wallets and cross-border digital payment solutions are gaining momentum in the countries reviewed. The Bank of Mongolia integrated international mobile payment systems, such as Apple Pay in December 2024, into the national payment ecosystem. The service was introduced through collaboration between the Ministry of Digital Development, Innovation and Communications, the Bank of Mongolia, Golomt Bank and the Trade and Development Bank. It allows users to make payments using Apple devices and supports international payments through the national "₮ Card". That development marks a significant step in modernizing the country's payment infrastructure, enabling more than 1.6 million Apple users to access Apple Pay at more than 150,000 point-of-sale terminals across the country.

In the Pacific region, digital financial platforms, such as MyCash, which is available in Fiji, Samoa and Tonga, are playing a transformative role in reshaping the digital finance landscape. By enabling users to receive international remittances directly into their mobile wallets, these mobile money solutions are helping to bridge long-standing gaps left by traditional banking systems, particularly in remote and underserved areas.

The National Bank of Cambodia has strengthened its digital ecosystem by introducing two new features to the Bakong digital platform: Bakong Cross-Border, which extends the platform's reach by enabling seamless transactions with neighbouring countries, such as the Lao People's Democratic Republic, Thailand and Vietnam; and Bakong Tourist, which allows travellers to make QR code payments at more than 3.3 million locations across Cambodia – significantly reducing reliance on cash and the need to exchange foreign currency. By integrating those features, Bakong not only enhances the convenience and security of financial transactions, but also promotes the use of the Cambodian riel, supporting national efforts to reduce dollarization and accelerate the development of the country's digital economy.

Kenya continues to lead the way in digital payments and financial inclusion in Africa, serving as a continental benchmark for innovation in the financial services sector. In 2024, as part of its National Payments Strategy 2022–2025, the Central Bank of Kenya implemented several key initiatives, including:

- The successful transition of the Kenya Electronic Payment and Settlement System to the new Global Messaging Standard (ISO 20022), providing a robust foundation for integration with regional and international payment systems.
- The initial roll-out of the Fast Payment System – a sector-wide interoperable solution enabling instant transfers

across the entire financial ecosystem. An industry technical working group was established to oversee the implementation process, which began in November 2024.

- Preliminary steps to link the country's financial institutions with counterparts across the EAC and Common Market for Eastern and Southern Africa regions by interconnecting national RTGS systems. The Central Bank of Kenya is also exploring direct linkages to PAPSS to further strengthen regional financial integration (box 5).

Box 5
How the Pan-African Payment and Settlement System is revolutionizing intra-African mobile payments

As African Governments and central banks increasingly intensify efforts to modernize their economies and promote cashless transactions, the demand for a unified and efficient payment infrastructure has become more pressing. In response, PAPSS was launched in 2022 by the African Union, in collaboration with the African Export-Import Bank, as a strategic instrument to support the implementation of AfCFTA.

PAPSS directly addresses key barriers to intra-African trade by enabling instant cross-border payments in local currencies, significantly lowering transaction costs and reducing dependence on foreign currencies. By connecting central banks, fintechs and payment service providers across the continent, the system strengthens financial integration and enhances the capacity of countries to trade efficiently under the AfCFTA framework.

As at July 2025, PAPSS had seen substantial adoption across Africa, positioning it as a cornerstone of the continent's evolving digital trade ecosystem. It is currently:

- Backed by 16 national central banks, providing foundational support for its operations.
- Integrated with more than 150 commercial banks, facilitating broad access to cross-border payment services.
- Connected with 14 payment switches, improving interoperability between national financial systems.

Those integrations span multiple regions, including:

- West Africa: Gambia, Ghana, Guinea, Liberia, Nigeria and Sierra Leone. They have been part of PAPSS since its pilot phase in 2022.
- East Africa: Kenya and Rwanda. They have adopted the system, with KCB Group and Bank of Kigali pioneering integration efforts.
- Southern Africa: Zambia and Zimbabwe. They have also onboarded PAPSS, contributing to its growing continental reach.

In addition, five major African multinational commercial banking groups, Access Bank Group, Ecobank Group, KCB Group, Standard Bank Group and UBA Group, have signed memorandums of understanding to implement PAPSS across their subsidiaries, extending its footprint to nearly 40 countries. Those developments underscore the critical role of PAPSS in enhancing financial integration and enabling seamless cross-border transactions across the continent. Looking ahead, PAPSS is well positioned to serve as a foundational element of Africa's financial infrastructure, supporting seamless cross-border trade, enhancing economic resilience and contributing to the realization of a single, integrated African market within AfCFTA.

Source: UNCTAD, based on information sourced from https://papss.com.

At the regional level, the EAC Cross-Border Payment System Masterplan was officially adopted in May 2025 by the EAC Monetary Affairs Committee, comprising central bank governors from Burundi, Kenya, Rwanda, Somalia, South Sudan, Uganda and the United Republic of Tanzania. That adoption marks a significant milestone in the region's efforts to modernize and integrate payment systems. By enabling seamless, real-time retail payments across borders, this strategic initiative is set to significantly strengthen cross-border interoperability and facilitate greater regional trade integration. As part of broader regional efforts, the African Confederation of Cooperative Savings and Credit Associations has joined forces with Visa to launch the Financial Inclusion in Kenya and Tanzania Project in 2024, aimed at delivering innovative, affordable financial services to underserved populations, particularly women and youth, while leveraging the capacity of participating cooperative societies.

D. Fostering a level playing field and rules-based ecosystem

Weak or fragmented legal foundations constrain the ability of MSMEs to engage confidently in e-commerce and digital trade.

As digital economies continue to evolve, regulatory frameworks must strike a balance between protecting consumers and businesses and enabling innovation and private sector participation. In many countries, however, progress is hampered by weak or fragmented legal foundations, outdated legislation, limited enforcement capacity and low levels of awareness among consumers and businesses. Those gaps constrain the ability of the private sector – particularly MSMEs – to engage confidently in digital trade. Furthermore, the widespread presence of informal markets, in which regulation is minimal and legal certainty is lacking, further increases risks and discourages formal sector growth.

Policy imbalances that favour regulation over facilitation risk stifling innovation and constraining private sector development.

While many Governments have taken steps to adopt e-commerce laws and pursue regional harmonization, these efforts at times lead to overregulation with a focus on sector-specific rules rather than the creation of a broader, enabling legal environment that supports innovation and the uptake of e-commerce and digital trade. Key legal foundations, such as frameworks for electronic transactions, digital identities and cross-border interoperability, remain underdeveloped or inconsistently applied. That policy imbalance, favouring regulation over facilitation, risks stifling innovation, constraining private sector development and limiting progress towards inclusive digital transformation.

In Africa, Togo is carrying out a comprehensive reform of its e-commerce regulatory framework to better reflect the changing digital ecosystem. In February 2025, the Ministry of Trade, Handicrafts and Local Consumption organized a workshop in Lomé to gather inputs from key stakeholders and refine the existing framework. That initiative is part of a broader technical support project aimed at assisting SMEs engaged in e-commerce.[51] The goal is to equip Togo with a modern, coherent legal framework that aligns with both regional and international standards. The workshop brought together representatives from public institutions, the private sector, online commerce operators and civil society, reflecting a multi-stakeholder approach to fostering a secure, consumer-friendly and well-regulated digital trade environment. In June 2024, Malawi enacted the Data Protection Act, aligning the legislation with constitutional privacy rights and international standards. To support its implementation, the Malawi Communications Regulatory Authority issued a compliance handbook

[51] The initiative is supported by the Arab-Africa Trade Bridges Programme and implemented by the International Islamic Trade Finance Corporation.

in which it summarizes key provisions and provides practical guidance for businesses and stakeholders.

East African countries are advancing comprehensive digital regulatory frameworks, as part of broader regional efforts to establish coherent and harmonized legal standards for the evolving digital economy. The United Republic of Tanzania is seeking technical support to benchmark best practices in regulatory frameworks for the development of e-commerce policies, laws and regulations. Similarly, Uganda is working towards a comprehensive legal framework to govern e-commerce covering issues related to consumer protection, intellectual property and taxation of online businesses, while establishing clear guidelines for cross-border e-commerce. Rwanda adopted its revised Competition and Consumer Protection Policy in September 2023, to better reflect the evolving dynamics of digital markets and cross-border trade.[52] The updated policy is aimed at enhancing regulatory oversight in e-commerce, digital financial services and emerging online platforms, while also addressing anti-competitive practices and green investments in the digital economy. In line with regional integration efforts, Rwanda is also aligning its consumer protection measures with the EAC framework, ensuring greater consistency and cooperation across borders. Ongoing capacity-building and stakeholder engagement are further strengthening the implementation of the revised policy (box 6).

In Asia, the E-commerce Act of Nepal, enacted in April 2025, marks a significant step towards strengthening consumer protection and establishing a clearer regulatory framework for digital trade. The law, which mandates registration for domestic and foreign digital sellers, responds to long-standing concerns from both businesses and consumers by formally recognizing social media platforms as legitimate e-commerce channels, introducing specific provisions to support SMEs and establishing a clearer legal framework for contractual agreements between sellers and platform operators.

In the Pacific region, Governments are increasingly acknowledging the importance of cybersecurity legislation to support a safe and secure digital transformation. In August 2024, Solomon Islands launched its first-ever cybersecurity policy aimed at creating a secure and resilient cyberenvironment. The policy is aligned with international best practices and includes the establishment of a dedicated working group to guide its implementation. In Tonga, five laws related to e-commerce are currently under revision by the relevant agencies, covering key areas such as electronic transactions, data protection and privacy, cybercrime and cybersecurity, consumer protection and e-payments.[53] Meanwhile, other Pacific island countries, such as Fiji and Vanuatu, have initiated legislative reviews to strengthen their cybersecurity frameworks, including drafting or updating laws on cybercrime and data protection. The Commonwealth is actively supporting those efforts by providing technical assistance and raising public awareness, particularly in the context of upcoming e-commerce legislation. Those developments mark an important step towards building trust in digital services and safeguarding users in an increasingly connected region.

[52] The new law on competition and consumer protection is currently being discussed in Parliament.

[53] The consumer protection bill is in the final draft stages and is awaiting submission to the Office of the Attorney General for translation. The electronic payment bill, developed in February 2025 with the assistance of the Pacific Agreement on Closer Economic Relations (PACER) Plus, is being reviewed internally before stakeholders' consultations.

Box 6
Revising e-commerce-related laws in the East African Community

As digital trade gains momentum across Africa, EAC is taking specific steps to modernize and harmonize its e-commerce regulatory frameworks. With rapid digital transformation reshaping how trade is conducted, particularly through online platforms and mobile technologies, the need for updated and cohesive laws has become increasingly urgent. To address those challenges, EAC, through its Competition Authority and in partnership with international development partners, is spearheading efforts to develop tailored regulations that reflect the evolving realities of the digital economy. One of the key initiatives includes support from GIZ to develop consumer protection regulations specifically for e-commerce, an area that the current EAC Competition Act does not adequately address. The Competition Authority is leading those efforts, with planned amendments to the existing framework to incorporate digital trade dimensions such as online advertising, platform liability and consumer rights in digital marketplaces. GIZ is also supporting a regional situational analysis of national e-transactions laws, with the goal of harmonizing legal provisions across EAC partner States to enhance legal predictability and foster cross-border digital trade.

Further bolstering those efforts, the World Bank has allocated $50 million under the East Africa Regional Integration Project, launched in 2023 and spanning five years. The Project is focused on regulatory harmonization of e-commerce-related laws across five main pillars, namely: (a) the development of laws, regulations and public-private partnership guidelines for enhancing regional digital connectivity; (b) data governance and protection, with the goal of harmonizing guidelines on data protection interoperability and managing cross-border data flows in accordance with international standards; (c) the development of a regional cybersecurity framework, with assessments currently under way; (d) the harmonization of digital payment systems and e-signature regulations, which are critical for building a trusted, unified regional digital identity and transaction environment; and (e) e-taxation frameworks, which are key to creating fair and efficient digital markets. As at May 2025, the project had piloted innovative cross-border mechanisms for secure data transfer and information-sharing, while promoting regional online market integration through the harmonization of payments and e-commerce frameworks. Capacity-building and awareness-raising activities are also planned for 2025 to complement those efforts.

Together, those initiatives reflect the strategic commitment of EAC to building a forward-looking regulatory environment that enables inclusive, secure and integrated e-commerce across the region. The harmonization of those legal frameworks not only supports regional integration but also positions EAC as a more competitive and cohesive digital trade bloc.

Source: UNCTAD.

While consumer protection and trust remain challenges for many developing countries, innovative approaches and legal reforms are emerging to empower consumers and build safer, more transparent digital economies. Leveraging digital tools, such as mobile applications, can empower consumers with information, facilitate complaints and enhance market transparency. Kenya offers a strong example of how public-private partnerships can enhance consumer protection in the digital economy. Through the success of M-Pesa, regulators and Safaricom have implemented safeguards to combat fraud, promote transparency and strengthen consumer trust in digital platforms. Rwanda is also making strides to build trust among online consumers. In 2024, 38 e-commerce platforms were certified with the Trust Seal certificate by the ICT Chamber, in line with relevant laws and regulations. The initiative was supported by the GIZ Pan-African E-commerce Initiative, which is working with institutions in other African countries to develop similar systems. In July 2024, the Parliament of Bangladesh passed the Payment and Settlement System Act, 2024, to mitigate risks in financial transactions and safeguard consumer interests by regulating, integrating, and overseeing payment and settlement systems. Earlier, in February 2023, the Government had also launched the Central Complaint Management System to protect consumers' rights and prevent e-commerce fraud.

As many developing countries revise their e-commerce laws, strengthening enforcement mechanisms and improving market oversight are key to ensuring that new regulations are effectively implemented. Efforts to increase awareness and knowledge play a crucial role in that regard. Samoa hosted a training session in 2024 for policymakers on legal instruments for e-commerce, funded by the PIF secretariat. The training aimed to enhance the capacity of public officials to better understand and implement digital trade policies.

Some countries are conducting legislative gap analyses to identify shortcomings and recommend reforms to strengthen their e-commerce legal frameworks. Jordan carried out a comprehensive regulatory impact assessment in 2023 with the support of the United States Agency for International Development, while Zambia is planning to conduct a needs assessment to identify regulatory overlaps and gaps and establish an online registry for e-commerce businesses. Similarly, Vanuatu is carrying out a legal gap analysis in 2025, supported by the Commonwealth, to address legal shortcomings and ensure that regulations align with evolving digital trade needs. A comprehensive cyberlaw gap analysis for 15 Pacific small island developing States was recently conducted by UNCTAD (2025e), in which it highlighted significant gaps in the region's digital legal frameworks, including outdated laws on data protection, consumer rights and e-commerce, which undermined trust and hindered digital trade. As digital adoption rapidly increases, UNCTAD emphasized the need for harmonized and comprehensive legal systems. While progress is being made, particularly on cybercrime legislation, coordinated efforts are still required to establish the legal frameworks essential for a secure, inclusive and trustworthy digital transformation.[54]

Emerging technologies, such as AI, blockchain and the Internet of things, are reshaping economic and social systems and hold significant potential to boost digital transformation. There is no global consensus, however, on what constitutes an adequate legal and regulatory framework for emerging technologies, although there have been some recent international cooperation developments in this area (e.g. G20 and OECD), including at the regional level (AfCFTA, ASEAN and the European Union). In two recent studies, the United Nations Commission on International Trade Law (UNCITRAL) concluded that most existing legal frameworks could accommodate their use, provided that general principles such as technology neutrality and functional equivalence were maintained.[55] Notwithstanding, emerging technologies do present regulatory and ethical challenges, particularly around data privacy, intellectual property, cybersecurity and liability. The premature adoption of technology-specific regulations without a solid legal foundation risks creating further fragmentation, reducing interoperability and hindering cross-border trade digitalization. That underscores the need for coherent, flexible, forward-looking legal systems that enable innovation while ensuring trust, legal certainty and alignment with international norms.

> Coherent, flexible and forward-looking legal systems should enable innovation while ensuring trust, legal certainty and alignment with international norms.

In Africa, Kenya is setting the stage for regulation of AI, by having introduced the Kenya Robotics and Artificial Intelligence Society Bill in 2023 and aligning it with international best practices.[56] The legislative

[54] The study was funded by the Government of Australia and developed by UNCTAD within the framework of the Pacific Digital Economy Programme.

[55] UNCITRAL (2025a and 2025b).

[56] These include the OECD Principles on Artificial Intelligence (adopted in 2019), ISO standards on AI and the European Union Artificial Intelligence Act, which are widely recognized as transparent, ethical and human-centric AI regulations.

proposal aims to regulate AI and robotics entities by licensing AI operators and enforcing penalties, including imprisonment, for violations. The Government also co-sponsored the first-ever United Nations resolution on AI regulation adopted in 2024, further demonstrating its commitment to advancing equitable AI policies on the global stage. To strengthen its position as a regional AI hub, the Government of Kenya launched its Artificial Intelligence Strategy 2025–2030 in May 2025, which is focused on promoting ethical and inclusive AI adoption and strengthening data governance mechanisms.

In Mauritania, the Ministry of Digital Transformation, Innovation and Modernization of the Administration finalized the country's National Artificial Intelligence Strategy (2025–2029) in July 2024. The strategy outlines six strategic priorities: developing human skills in AI, promoting research and innovation, enhancing regional and international collaboration, establishing data governance for AI, bolstering international connectivity and addressing ethical issues in AI. It also includes specific projects to apply AI across key development sectors, such as healthcare, education, agriculture, fishing, transport, energy and defence. Similarly, Zambia launched its National Artificial Intelligence Strategy 2024–2026 in November 2024, developed in collaboration with the Tony Blair Institute and the Government of Finland. The Strategy seeks to harness AI for economic growth, improve public service delivery and foster innovation in priority areas, including education, agriculture and healthcare.

In Asia, Mongolia is advancing the integration of AI and big data into its economy, governance and public services. The Government is focused on leveraging those technologies to drive sector-wide innovation, support a fair and sustainable digital transition and ensure strong cross-sectoral coordination. As part of that effort, in February 2025, the Ministry of Digital Development, Innovation and Communications of Mongolia, in partnership with UNDP, organized the country's first-ever conference on a national strategy for big data and AI. The event convened government officials, industry leaders and international experts to shape the country's approach to AI and digital transformation, laying the foundation for a future national strategy.

Developing national AI strategies and policies will be crucial in the coming years to ensure that countries harness the benefits of these emerging technologies while mitigating associated risks. A well-defined strategy can provide a regulatory framework that promotes ethical AI use, safeguards privacy and human rights and addresses biases and existing inequalities. For developing countries, such strategies also offer a pathway to leapfrog traditional development hurdles by leveraging AI for economic growth and development. Without a clear road map, those nations risk becoming passive consumers of AI technologies shaped by external powers, thus missing out on the opportunity to shape their digital futures and ensure equitable technological advancement. To address that challenge, the Commission on Science and Technology for Development advocates for tailored technical assistance, multi-stakeholder engagement and international cooperation to empower developing countries in establishing robust AI ecosystems aligned with their unique development priorities and socioeconomic contexts. Such support is essential to ensure that those nations are not left behind but become active participants in the global AI governance landscape, maximizing the technology's potential for sustainable and inclusive growth.

E. Strengthening digital skills and e-commerce business development

As digital transformation reshapes economies and societies, education systems are evolving to equip individuals, businesses and Governments with essential digital skills. Digital competencies – from basic digital literacy to advanced skills related to data analysis, AI use, cloud computing and software development – form the backbone of productivity, innovation and competitiveness in the digital age. Those skills empower individuals to participate meaningfully in the digital economy, enable businesses to innovate and scale, and allow public institutions to deliver more efficient, inclusive and transparent services. However, developing countries continue to face challenges in acquiring those capabilities, due to limited access to quality education and training, insufficient digital infrastructure and gaps in policy or institutional frameworks to support lifelong learning and upskilling. To achieve truly inclusive digitalization, efforts must go beyond connectivity by addressing foundational skills development. Many digital platforms and services remain inaccessible to those with low literacy levels or who speak local languages, especially in rural and underserved areas. Building digital skills – from basic literacy to advanced competencies in AI and data – is essential, but without tackling barriers, such as language, education quality and access to relevant content, digital trade and e-commerce initiatives risk deepening existing inequalities. Rural-urban divides and gender disparities further exacerbate inequalities in digital skill acquisition.

Another critical challenge in digital markets is the risk of deskilling and worker dissatisfaction arising from mismatches between qualifications and available jobs. A recent study indicates that highly educated workers in developing countries are often relegated to relatively low-skill tasks, including text and image annotation or content moderation.[57] Even with a well-educated workforce, insufficient opportunities for high-skill employment can lead to underutilization of talent, frustration and ultimately brain drain, as workers seek better prospects elsewhere. Addressing that requires not only expanding digital job creation but also ensuring alignment between workforce skills and the complexity and value of the tasks offered.

To address those issues, many reviewed countries are integrating digital technologies into national education curricula – updating teaching content, investing in teacher training and embedding digital literacy from an early age. In Senegal, the Ministry of National Education is leading a pioneering initiative to integrate digital skills into school curricula through the PROMET project, piloted in 2024 in the Pikine-Guédiawaye education district. Focused on introducing students to algorithmic thinking and computer programming, the project has brought digital education and coding to all 42 lower secondary schools in the district. More than 100 teachers have been trained in interactive, student-centred teaching methods, benefiting more than 10,000 students to date. Complementing those efforts, the DigiTruk initiative is an example of successful multi-stakeholder partnership in Senegal, led by Huawei under the global Tech4All digital inclusion programme. Implemented in collaboration with Sonatel, various government ministries and the non-governmental organization Close the Gap, the initiative offers free, high-quality digital training in underserved areas, equipping Senegalese youth with essential digital skills. By the end of 2024, the initiative had reached more than 3,100 young people across 28 communes in

> Without tackling barriers such as language, education quality and access to relevant content, digital trade and e-commerce risk deepening existing inequalities.

[57] UNCTAD (2025f, chap. II, sect. G).

seven regions, with women accounting for 56 per cent of the participants.

To address the shortage of skilled ICT professionals, the Government of Solomon Islands launched, in 2024, a two-year junior professional programme, supported by the Australian Solomon Islands Partnership for Governance. The initiative, designed in six-month learning cycles, seeks to provide a strong foundation in essential ICT skills and industry-relevant knowledge through blended training, workshops and mentorship. After completing the six-month programme, junior professionals may be recruited into the public service as ICT professionals.

Mauritania has also taken important steps to reform its education system by integrating digital technologies into national curricula. In January 2025, the Ministry of Education and System Reform convened a workshop with key stakeholders to develop a national road map for digital transformation in education. The aim is to establish a clear development strategy that will serve as the foundation for a modern, inclusive and sustainable education system. That effort is part of the country's broader Digital Transformation Strategy and follows its recent participation in the FIFA Foundation's Digital Education Programme – which is aimed at improving the digital and life skills of young people, through football-themed activities – making it the first African nation to join. Over the next three years, the plan is to train 10,000 children aged 6 to 12 in coding, robotics and digital literacy. If effectively carried out, the road map will support equitable and coherent technology integration to enhance access, quality and learning outcomes in the education sector of Mauritania.

The private sector is playing an active role in building digital skills to facilitate the growth of e-commerce and broader digital business development. Chambers of commerce, industry associations and leading private enterprises are investing in innovative training programmes aimed at equipping entrepreneurs, SMEs and workers with the competencies needed to thrive in a digital marketplace. Kenya has emerged as a strong example in that area. In February 2025, a high-impact sensitization workshop was organized by the Kenya National Chamber of Commerce and Industry, in collaboration with the Kenya Association of Manufacturers and TradeMark Africa. The workshop brought together 54 Kenyan SMEs from five different counties in the coastal region, to learn how to leverage e-commerce and AfCFTA for business expansion. Participants reported having gained first-hand knowledge on how to use the Isoko e-commerce platform[58] to access markets across Africa. Twenty businesses were successfully onboarded onto the platform, setting the stage for seamless cross-border transactions. The workshop featured discussions on export strategies, trade regulations and digital solutions, ensuring SMEs are equipped to compete within the AfCFTA framework. The University of Nairobi recently organized four hackathons, bringing together 69 multidisciplinary student teams to pitch creative solutions to real-world challenges. Designed to foster business development and start-up thinking, the event showcased a vibrant culture of innovation and entrepreneurship and served as a launchpad for future entrepreneurs through hands-on workshops in design thinking, business modelling and innovation around a safe e-commerce environment.

In Senegal, the Cheikh Hamidou Kane Digital University, in partnership with the Mastercard Foundation, launched the FORCE-N programme, in 2021, dedicated to the development of employment and employability of young people in the digital sector. The six-year programme supports the country's digital transformation by equipping young people with skills for careers in six key technology fields, including software development, AI and data, e-business, digital content creation and cybersecurity.

58 The platform was developed by TradeMark Africa with funding from Global Affairs Canada.

It offers approximately 30 certifications tailored to the needs of Senegalese businesses and the global job market. Its component on science, technology, engineering and mathematics supports excellence in science and digital education in secondary schools by equipping laboratories, distributing computers and offering an online learning platform. It also promotes digital culture through activities such as robotics, astronomy, coding and three-dimensional printing. Since its launch, 14,525 young people have been trained under the programme in essential digital skills, 10,402 have been supported in securing employment post-certification and seven digital start-ups have been created as a result.[59]

Development partners are also increasingly supporting e-commerce business development and digital skills building. In Tunisia, the ecomConnect Hub was established in 2023 with the support of ITC to strengthen the capacities of local e-commerce operators, especially in remote and underserved regions. By providing practical tools, training and market-relevant knowledge, the initiative has already reached more than 500 participants through webinars, in-person events and self-paced online courses on essential e-commerce skills, including cross-border e-commerce, digital platforms, logistics, payment systems and regulatory frameworks. Similarly, the SMART Zambia Institute, in collaboration with the National Institute for Public Administration and ITU, conducted four digital skills training sessions on essential digital skills for more than 40 participants, including out-of-school youth.[60]

Business incubators and innovation hubs are driving digital skills development and have expanded steadily in recent years, supported by Governments, development partners and the private sector. That growth reflects increasing recognition of their role in fostering innovation-driven entrepreneurship, especially in emerging sectors such as fintech, agricultural technology, green technologies and creative industries. From urban innovation hubs to rural-focused incubators, those initiatives are helping to build more inclusive digital economies by unlocking local talent and strengthening the entrepreneurial ecosystem at the grass-roots level.

Among the countries under review, the Ministry of Production of Peru has allocated funds to establish three new business incubators in the regions of Cuzco, Huánuco and San Martín, to support the development of innovative start-ups and high-impact business models.[61] The funding, awarded through the ProInnóvate programme in October 2024, will help the incubators improve their technical and management capabilities, benefiting local entrepreneurs. The initiative is expected to generate employment, attract capital for start-ups and drive innovation in the local economies.

In Vanuatu, the V-Lab incubator continues to play a pivotal role in empowering young entrepreneurs, especially in the green economy and innovation sectors. Since its establishment in 2019, V-Lab had supported more than 470 individuals as at November 2024, through personalized coaching, financial assistance and access to a dynamic network of mentors. It regularly hosts events that connect aspiring entrepreneurs with industry leaders. Another key contributor to the country's growing incubation ecosystem is the Innovation and Digital Economy Association. In 2024, the Association and V-Lab co-organized a workshop – backed by the Department of Industry and the Vanuatu Chamber of Commerce and Industry – to increase the participation of local businesses in online markets. Complementing those efforts, the ITU Smart Islands programme has extended digital financial literacy to remote

Business incubators and innovation hubs foster innovation-driven entrepreneurship, especially in emerging sectors such as fintech, agricultural technology, green technologies and creative industries.

[59] See https://force-n.sn/en/about-us.

[60] The programme is supported by the Norwegian Agency for Development Cooperation.

[61] The three winners of the second edition of the Innovative Business Incubators and Accelerators competition were Incuval Ventures (Huánuco), BioInnova (San Martín), and Idea Lab (Cuzco); each received up to approximately $183,000 in grants.

communities. Through hands-on workshops conducted between January 2023 and December 2024, which were led by local mobile service providers, residents in South Malekula have started using digital wallets, thus reducing their reliance on costly travel to urban centres for financial transactions.

The PIF secretariat has also been instrumental in advancing e-commerce skills and digital business development across the region, in line with the Pacific Regional E-commerce Strategy and Roadmap. In September 2024, the secretariat concluded its E-Biz Plus pilot initiative, which was aimed at strengthening the e-commerce readiness of MSMEs in Micronesia (Federated States of), Samoa, Tuvalu and Vanuatu. The initiative provided expert-led training, practical toolkits and small grants. More than 77 businesses benefited from the training, with 8 selected for additional support. Since the initiative's launch in late 2023, participating businesses have reported notable improvements: for example, Hard Rock Sokehs (Federated States of Micronesia) reported tripling its sales after the launch of its e-commerce site; O-Tahiti Pearls (Samoa) saw a 20 per cent increase in sales following marketing upgrades; and firms such as Talofa Studios and Malekula Island Organic improved their business strategies and online visibility. Building on that success, the initiative was expanded to Niue and Tonga in 2024 and is set to launch in Kiribati in 2025.[62]

Equipping learners with AI-driven skills, including digital and e-commerce capabilities, provides youth, SMEs, and educators with opportunities in online trade.

AI is offering new opportunities to national education systems in many developing countries by boosting learning outcomes, bridging teaching gaps and promoting inclusivity. Globally, AI is revolutionizing the education system through its ability to personalize learning experiences and address disparities in access to knowledge. However, the extent of its impact depends on key enablers, such as digital infrastructure, teacher training and inclusive governance frameworks. Without those foundations, AI may risk deepening existing inequalities.

The importance of building AI-related skills is also reflected in UNCTAD frontier technology readiness index, which benchmarks countries' preparedness to adopt and leverage a range of frontier technologies, including AI, robotics, blockchain and green technologies. The index assesses capabilities across five key dimensions – ICT infrastructure, human capital, industrial capacity, research and development and policy environment – providing a composite ranking of economies' readiness. Several of the countries reviewed in the present report feature in the latest rankings, highlighting varying levels of preparedness to integrate AI into their education systems and broader digital strategies. Such comparative insights can help identify priority areas for investment, capacity-building and policy reform to ensure that the benefits of frontier technologies are widely shared and equitably distributed.[63]

In Africa, countries such as Ghana, Kenya, Rwanda and Tunisia are among the most prepared to harness the potential of AI, according to the AI Preparedness Index, which was recently developed by the International Monetary Fund.[64] Kenya, in particular, is emerging as a leader with its national AI strategy, the implementation of AI-powered educational technology solutions and strategic partnerships with major technology firms. Building on the country's technology ecosystem, Microsoft launched a major skilling initiative in 2024 to train 1 million people in AI and cybersecurity by 2027, in alignment with Kenya Vision 2030 and its Digital Master Plan. The initiative is not only enhancing general education but also equipping learners with job-ready digital skills, including e-commerce skills. Through platforms such as the Kenya Skills Hub, the Smart Academy and the Ajira

[62] The initiative is supported by Australia, the European Union and the Commonwealth, under the broader Pacific E-commerce Initiative and the 2050 Strategy for the Blue Pacific Continent.

[63] UNCTAD (2025f).

[64] See https://www.imf.org/en/Blogs/Articles/2024/06/25/mapping-the-worlds-readiness-for-artificial-intelligence-shows-prospects-diverge.

and Jitume centres, the initiative empowers youth, SMEs, educators and underserved communities to adopt and apply AI-driven solutions in real-world contexts, including online entrepreneurship, digital trade and business process outsourcing. Comprehensive AI education efforts are being rolled out across all levels – from schools to universities and vocational centres – supported by initiatives such as university tours and faculty immersion programmes, to build a robust pipeline of talent for the digital transformation agenda.

In January 2025, Ghana hosted its first national workshop on AI in teacher education, supported by the Commonwealth of Learning. The workshop brought together educators and officials to explore the transformative potential of AI in modernizing teacher training and promoting educational equality. Similarly, the Government of Rwanda is currently working to enhance the skills of educators by training lecturers from various tertiary institutions across the country in the effective use of AI. The initiative is aimed at empowering both educators and students with the skills needed to incorporate AI into teaching and learning practices. A national data-sharing framework is set to be introduced in 2025, enabling institutions, including the Ministry of Education, to share data responsibly, fostering collaboration between the public and private sectors to advance AI-powered tools and solutions.

In April 2024, Tunisia announced plans to establish its first public institute specialized in AI at the University of Tunis, starting from the next academic year. The institute aims to broaden the areas in which AI can be used in Tunisia and ensure its proper use, while protecting citizens' personal data. In September 2024, Tunisia launched a new AI Innovation Hub in Novation City, a technology park designed to foster a dynamic innovation ecosystem. Developed in collaboration with the NVIDIA Deep Learning Institute, the Hub provides training, cutting-edge technologies and access to business networks to accelerate AI adoption, with a goal of training 100,000 developers across Africa over the next three years.

Despite the promise of AI to enhance educational outcomes, significant challenges remain, particularly in ensuring equitable access in areas with poor connectivity, addressing cultural barriers to adoption, and developing inclusive, ethical frameworks that preserve human agency and promote critical thinking. UNCTAD (2025f) has highlighted the transformative potential of AI, estimating a $4.8 trillion global impact, but warns of widening digital divides. While AI tools have the potential to enhance learning efficiency and save time for both teachers and students, their benefits are unevenly distributed – especially in areas in which Internet connectivity is limited or unreliable, exacerbating existing educational inequalities. In addition, cultural barriers to technology adoption further slowdown efforts to build AI-related skills. To harness the transformative potential of AI in education responsibly and equitably, policymakers must prioritize long-term capacity-building, teacher training and the development of culturally sensitive, inclusive frameworks. Strengthening governance with clear ethical guidelines and fostering interdisciplinary collaboration are essential to ensure that AI enhances, rather than replaces, human learning, while promoting critical thinking, creativity and social equity.

To harness the transformative potential of AI in education responsibly and equitably, policymakers must prioritize long-term capacity-building, teacher training and culturally sensitive, inclusive frameworks.

F. Improving access to finance for digital entrepreneurs

Limited early-stage venture capital and stringent collateral requirements continue to constrain access to finance for digital entrepreneurs.

Despite the expansion of the digital economy, entrepreneurs across many of the countries reviewed continue to face significant barriers to accessing finance, particularly in the early stages of business development. A common key challenge identified by eT Readies is the limited availability of early-stage venture capital, stringent collateral requirements from financial institutions and regulatory frameworks that are not yet fully supportive of digital business models. Those constraints are compounded by systemic issues, such as fragmented regulations, emerging digital payment ecosystems and limited familiarity among investors and regulators with the dynamics of digital entrepreneurship. In response, Governments and regional bodies are stepping up with targeted initiatives to bridge the financing gap and foster a more supportive ecosystem for digital start-ups.

In 2024, Mauritania established the National Guarantee Fund and an Innovation Fund to enhance access to finance for young entrepreneurs. Those Funds are aimed at creating more than 10,000 financing opportunities for projects led by youth and women, including those operating in the e-commerce sector. Similar initiatives were implemented in other countries reviewed. In Zambia, the Innovation Programme of the Zambia Information and Communications Technology Authority offers access to finance, business support services and networking opportunities to digital start-ups and entrepreneurs. Key benefits include expert-led training workshops, mentorship with industry experts, access to technical testing devices and funding opportunities for commercialization or scale-up of innovative projects.

In Asia, Nepal launched the Nepal Impact Investment Community 2 Fund in August 2024, with $100 million of initial capital. The Fund seeks to invest in innovative SMEs operating in the technological space. Supported by the Swiss Agency for Development and Cooperation, the Fund pioneers a unique financing model in Nepal, blending debt and equity financing with technical assistance and business development support for technology and technology-enabled SMEs. Since its creation, the Fund has already received in excess of 65 applications from more than 15 sectors within just three months.

Bangladesh has made significant institutional progress in fostering innovation and entrepreneurship through the establishment of Startup Bangladesh Limited in 2020. As the country's first government-backed venture capital initiative, it was launched with an initial capital allocation of approximately $59 million to catalyse the growth of its start-up ecosystem. The initiative supports enterprises across all stages of development, ranging from pre-seed to growth, and operates as both a fund of funds and asset manager, offering not only capital but also strategic in-kind support to start-ups and ecosystem stakeholders. By 2024, the fund had deployed more than $7 million across 26 start-ups, achieving an aggregate two and a half times increase in portfolio valuation. Startup Bangladesh has also prioritized social and environmental considerations in its investment strategy, aligning its efforts with the Sustainable Development Goals.[65]

In an effort to formalize and streamline regulatory frameworks for start-ups, several countries have recently enacted or advanced start-up acts. In November 2023, Côte d'Ivoire adopted Act No. 2023-901, establishing a comprehensive framework that includes tax incentives, preferential access to public procurement, regulatory sandboxes and expanded mentorship and

65 See https://www.startupbangladesh.vc.

networking opportunities for emerging digital ventures. Similarly, in September 2023, Mauritania introduced its Start-up Act, marking a significant milestone in its digital development strategy. Officially promulgated in January 2024, the Act provides a dedicated legal foundation to support the growth of innovative, high-value-added SMEs. Over the next five years, it aims to certify 300 start-ups and strengthen a dozen entrepreneurship support structures. The Startup Bill in Kenya, introduced in 2021, is expected to be enacted by 2025. Uganda has a Start-up Policy under way, while Ghana is in the final stages of approving its Innovation and Startup Bill, which will establish a national agency and a fund to provide structured and financial support for new ventures.

Despite those legislative advancements, some countries are facing delays in implementing their start-up acts. Those setbacks are often linked to bureaucratic bottlenecks, limited institutional capacity and competing policy priorities. For example, in Senegal, the Ministry of Finance and Budget carried out an extended review process that contributed to a five-year gap between the enactment of the Start-up Act and the adoption of its implementing decree. That case underscores the importance of stronger interministerial coordination, enhanced institutional capacity and the development of time-bound implementation road maps to ensure timely and effective policy execution.

Regional initiatives to expand financial inclusion and strengthen fintech ecosystems are creating new pathways for digital entrepreneurs to access credit. In 2024, UNDP launched the second phase of its Timbuktoo initiative, aiming to enhance access to finance for digital and youth-led start-ups across Africa. The second phase is focused on mobilizing $1 billion in catalytic and commercial capital to support early-stage ventures, addressing the continent's significant gap in domestic risk capital. Key components include the establishment of eight thematic hubs in sectors such as fintech, healthcare technology, green technology and educational technology, alongside the expansion of university innovation pods across 13 countries to nurture local talent and innovation. Associated programmes such as the FinTech Startup Accelerator Programme offer equity-free funding of up to $25,000, as well as mentorship and investor networking opportunities, to selected start-ups. By integrating ecosystem development with targeted financial support, Timbuktoo is designed to empower young African entrepreneurs and stimulate job creation and digital transformation across the continent.

Inspired by regional experiences, Tonga is developing a Fintech regulatory sandbox framework to promote responsible innovation, aiming to provide a controlled environment for testing new financial technologies. Similarly, Tunisia is enhancing access to financial services by fostering partnerships with fintech companies to facilitate digital payments and financing, encouraging informal operators to transition into the formal economy. Despite the positive momentum for financial inclusion, developing countries still face major structural and operational challenges, such as insufficient incentives for private sector engagement, particularly in high-risk and low-return markets, fragmented and inconsistent digital market regulations that hinder cross-border investments and innovation and underdeveloped support ecosystems, including limited access to quality incubators, accelerators and mentorship networks. To address those barriers, Governments will need to actively promote blended finance models, work towards harmonizing regulatory frameworks and invest in capacity-building that improves the investment readiness of digital entrepreneurs.

> Blended finance models, regulatory harmonization and targeted capacitybuil ding are emerging as key strategies to improve the investment readiness of digital entrepreneurs.

Chapter III

Conclusion

Developing countries, particularly least developed countries, are progressing in various ways in building inclusive and resilient digital ecosystems, with the support of UNCTAD and other development partners. Across regions, countries have made notable strides in expanding Internet connectivity, enhancing digital services, modernizing logistics and transport networks and advancing payment solutions. Regulatory reforms are evolving to cover data protection, cybersecurity and e-commerce, while investments in digital skills, entrepreneurship and access to finance are helping individuals and MSMEs to engage more effectively in the digital economy. Together, those efforts are laying the groundwork for more connected, competitive and inclusive societies.

However, despite progress, digital transformation remains uneven and insufficient to sustain momentum or close critical gaps in e-commerce and digital trade readiness. Connectivity divides persist, especially in rural and remote areas. Logistics and payment systems are often fragmented and regulatory frameworks generally cannot keep up with the high pace of innovation. Many countries face structural challenges, including limited financing for start-ups, weak institutional capacities and difficulties enforcing newly adopted regulations. Equally critical is the need to address enabling conditions and foundational skills, without which digital inclusion efforts risk leaving the most vulnerable even further behind. Rapid technological change – driven by AI, data flows and digital platforms – makes addressing those gaps more difficult and more urgent than ever.

A recurring theme is the need for stronger political and institutional leadership to move from strategy to implementation. While many countries have adopted digital and e-commerce strategies, effective execution remains a challenge amid competing policy priorities, resource constraints and frequent shifts in government. Sustained political commitment is vital to embed digital transformation as a long-term development priority. At the institutional level, insufficient staffing, budget limitations and inadequate coordination mechanisms continue to hamper progress. Strengthening public sector capacity – especially among implementation units and lead agencies – is crucial, as is ensuring inclusive participation of women, youth and marginalized groups in digital policymaking.

Development cooperation in the digital domain is expanding, but concerns remain about its sustainability. Donor budget constraints, driven by domestic pressures, are prompting aid reallocations that may affect digital transformation support in least developed countries. Fragmented interventions and misaligned programming cycles further complicate coordination. Nonetheless, countries and partners alike recognize the importance of deepening collaboration, leveraging public-private partnerships, enhancing transparency and scaling resource mobilization. Tools such as the eTrade Reform Tracker offer opportunities to improve planning, monitoring and coordination.

Moving forward, more inclusive and evidence-based policymaking will be critical. Governments, development partners and the private sector share a collective responsibility to align reforms, bridge capacity gaps and ensure that efforts across policy areas – connectivity, logistics, regulation, finance and skills – are mutually reinforcing. The Global Digital Compact offers a timely framework for collective action, emphasizing the need to bridge digital divides and ensure that digitalization contributes meaningfully to broader development goals. With strong leadership, institutional resilience and international support, countries can accelerate their digital transformation journeys and realize the full potential of the digital economy for sustainable and inclusive development.

References

GSMA (2024). The State of the Industry Report on Mobile Money. London.

ITU (2024). Facts and Figures 2024. Geneva.

ITU, UNESCO and the Broadband Commission for Sustainable Development (2023). The State of Broadband 2023: Digital Connectivity – A Transformative Opportunity. ITU and UNESCO. Geneva.

Oughton EJ, Amaglobeli D and Moszoro M (2023). Estimating digital infrastructure investment needs to achieve universal broadband. Working Paper No. 23/27. International Monetary Fund.

UNCITRAL (2025a). Draft guidance document on legal issues relating to the use of distributed ledger technology in trade. A/CN.9/1222. Vienna. 2 May.

UNCITRAL (2025b). Legal issues relating to the use of decentralized autonomous organizations in trade. A/CN.9/1225. Vienna. 28 April.

UNCTAD (2020). Fast-Tracking Implementation of eTrade Readiness Assessments, first edition (United Nations publication. Sales No. E.20.II.D.34. Geneva).

UNCTAD (2021). Manual for the Production of Statistics on the Digital Economy 2020, revised edition (United Nations publication. Sales No. E.21.II.D.15. Geneva).

UNCTAD (2022a). Fast-Tracking Implementation of eTrade Readiness Assessments, second edition (United Nations publication. Sales No. E.22.II.D.21. Geneva).

UNCTAD (2022b). Member States of the Economic Community of West African States – eTrade Readiness Assessment (United Nations publication. Sales No. E.22.II.D.30. Geneva).

UNCTAD (2023a). Measuring the Value of E-commerce (United Nations publication. Sales No. E.23.II.D.5. Geneva).

UNCTAD (2023b). Fast-Tracking Implementation of eTrade Readiness Assessments, third edition (United Nations publication. Sales No. E.23.II.D.29. Geneva).

UNCTAD (2024a). Digital Economy Report 2024: Shaping an Environmentally Sustainable and Inclusive Digital Future (United Nations publication. Sales No. E.24.II.D.12. Geneva).

UNCTAD (2024b). Report of the Intergovernmental Group of Experts on E-commerce and the Digital Economy on its seventh session. TD/B/EDE/7/4 and TD/B/EDE/7/4/Corr.1. Geneva. 6 June 2024 and 21 March 2025, respectively.

UNCTAD (2025a). E-commerce and Digital Economy Programme: Year in Review 2024 (Geneva).

UNCTAD (2025b). Aid at the Crossroads: Trends in Official Development Assistance (Geneva).

UNCTAD (2025c). Indirect Taxation of E-commerce and Digital Trade: Implications for Developing Countries (United Nations publication. Sales No. E.23.II.D.4. Geneva).

UNCTAD (2025d). Digital Economy Report: Pacific Edition 2024. Promoting Digital Entrepreneurship and Trade (United Nations publication. Sales No. E.25.II.D.2. Geneva).

UNCTAD (2025e). Gap Analysis of Cyberlaws in Pacific Small Island Developing States (United Nations publication. Sales No. E.25.II.D.4. Geneva).

UNCTAD (2025f). Technology and Innovation Report 2025: Inclusive Artificial Intelligence for Development (United Nations publication. Sales No. E.25.II.D.1. Geneva).

United Nations (2023). Digital and Sustainable Trade Facilitation: Global Report 2023.

United Nations (2025), UN Global Survey on Digital and Sustainable Trade Facilitation 2025 (untfsurvey.org).

World Bank (2023). Connecting to Compete 2023: Trade Logistics in an Uncertain Global Economy – The Logistics Performance and its Indicators. Washington, D.C.

World Bank (2025). Global Findex Database 2025: Connectivity and Financial Inclusion in the Digital Economy. Washington, D.C.

Annex I

Case studies

A. Digital awakening in Cambodia: unlocking e-commerce potential in a young and connected nation

Cambodia, a South-East Asian country rich in cultural heritage and youthful dynamism, is in the midst of a digital transformation that is reshaping its economic landscape. With more than 65 per cent of the population under the age of 30, surging Internet penetration and growing smartphone adoption, Cambodia is fast becoming fertile ground for e-commerce. The coronavirus disease (COVID-19) pandemic further accelerated that shift, changing consumer behaviour and pushing both businesses and policymakers towards digital platforms. As Cambodia navigates its journey towards graduation from the category of least developed country and deeper global integration, digital trade is emerging as a central pillar of its economic strategy.

While e-commerce remains nascent – accounting for just 4 to 5 per cent of gross domestic product according to a recent report, it is expanding rapidly. Despite lagging behind some regional peers, the country's e-commerce accounts for approximately 12 to 13 per cent of the total for the Association of Southeast Asian Nations (ASEAN), highlighting significant untapped potential in a regional market worth $116.4 billion in 2024.1

1. Government vision for digital growth

The Government has placed digital transformation at the heart of its national development strategy. Through the Digital Economy and Society Policy Framework 2021–2035, the Digital Government Policy 2022–2035 and the Pentagonal Strategy Phase I (2023–2028), e-commerce is recognized as a key pillar for inclusive growth. Building on that foundation, the Ministry of Commerce is finalizing a Cambodia digital trade strategy (2025–2030) to strengthen digital inclusivity and international competitiveness. That strategic vision is supported by tangible actions: the launch of the Online Business Registration platform; a national data exchange platform, CamDX, for data interoperability between government systems; a platform designed to authenticate official government documents;2 and a business-to-business marketplace3 to help small and medium-sized enterprises (SMEs), especially women and youth entrepreneurs, enter the digital space. The launch of a national single window in 2024 marked a milestone for trade facilitation, enabling exporters and importers to submit standardized documents through a single portal – streamlining cross-border processes and aligning with ASEAN digital integration goals.

The groundwork for that transformation was laid early on, with the eTrade Readiness Assessment (eT Ready) in 2017 helping to define the country's e-commerce road map and design policy instruments on e-commerce and the digital economy. The country's E-commerce Strategy, formulated in 2020 with financial support from the Enhanced Integrated Framework (EIF), guides efforts to improve the overall e-commerce business environment and digital infrastructure, raise SME capabilities, enhance digital skills and domestic and cross-border logistics, develop a responsive skills infrastructure for e-commerce and expand the e-commerce ecosystem into rural areas.

[1] See https://api.techostartup.center/media/files/PROFITENCE_2024_E-commerce_Report_2.pdf.
[2] See https://verify.gov.kh.
[3] See https://cambodiatrade.com.

2. Youth powering the digital shift

The country's youthful and technology-savvy population is driving the rapid rise of e-commerce. By 2024, there were around 21.9 million mobile subscriptions and 20 million Internet connections, reflecting near-universal smartphone access. Urban hubs have become centres of digital innovation, in which young entrepreneurs and digital-first consumers embrace online platforms for commerce, communication and creativity. Social media channels serve as key entry points for small businesses to market and sell products directly to consumers, often substituting traditional e-commerce platforms.

That youth-led momentum is being supported by national initiatives aimed at building capacity and closing digital divides. Programmes such as the Techo Startup Center and Go4eCAM (EIF-funded e-commerce development project) provide micro-, small and medium-sized enterprises (MSMEs) and young entrepreneurs with training, digital tools and access to government-backed platforms to scale their businesses. Those initiatives prioritize inclusion, supporting women and rural entrepreneurs to participate in the digital economy. Complementing those efforts, the Cambodia Skills Development Roadmap (2023–2035) fosters lifelong learning and workforce digitalization, laying the foundation for a robust, future-ready e-commerce ecosystem.

3. From cash only to digital by default

Among the country's most notable digital successes is the surge in digital payments. Nationwide QR-code payments have massively ramped up with 601 million transactions in 2023. The Bakong instant payment system has also strengthened cross-border links: in 2024, Bakong integrated with Alipay+ and partnered with Maybank (Malaysia) and JB Financial (Republic of Korea), easing international transfers. New Bakong services include a tourist application (launched in 2024) that lets foreign visitors pay at more than 3.3 million outlets using a QR code. Buy-now-pay-later services are also emerging: banks are partnering with e-commerce platforms to offer interest-free instalment loans, further embedding digital finance in online shopping.

4. Policy and legal foundations

Cambodia has also been active in building a robust legal and regulatory framework to foster trust and safety in online transactions. The Law on Electronic Commerce (2019) and the Law on Consumer Protection (2019) laid the groundwork for secure transactions. Cybersecurity and data protection laws, currently under development, will seek to address privacy and cybercrime concerns, while the introduction of the Cambodia E-commerce Trustmark System has enhanced consumer confidence through verified online businesses.

On the regional front, Cambodia is aligning with ASEAN e-commerce initiatives, including participation in the Digital Economy Framework Agreement negotiations. The country has also signed bilateral trade agreements with major digital economies, including China and the Republic of Korea, and is deepening digital cooperation through the Comprehensive Economic Partnership Agreement with the United Arab Emirates.

5. Ongoing challenges and lessons learned

Despite such progress, Cambodia continues to face key challenges. Connectivity remains uneven, especially in rural areas, with an estimated 74 per cent of the rural population suffering from poor Internet connectivity. Digital literacy gaps persist among SMEs and many businesses still lack a formal online presence. High levels of informality, weak consumer trust and insufficient dispute resolution mechanisms slow down e-commerce adoption. Interoperability between government platforms needs strengthening and more cohesive private sector representation is needed to effectively advocate for policy improvements.

However, the country's e-commerce journey offers valuable lessons. Effective coordination among ministries led by the Ministry of Commerce, with support from development partners, such as United Nations Conference on Trade and Development (UNCTAD), the International Trade Centre (ITC), the United Nations Development Programme (UNDP) and the German Agency for International Cooperation (GIZ), has enabled strategic alignment and policy coherence. The focus is now to start shifting from domestic digital integration to cross-border e-commerce readiness, ensuring that MSMEs can scale and access international markets and reach out to overseas consumers.

6. Sustaining momentum and scaling innovation

Looking ahead, the e-commerce ecosystem appears poised for expansion as infrastructure and policies mature. By addressing rural connectivity and digital literacy gaps, strengthening consumer protection and leveraging e-commerce trends, Cambodia can accelerate its digital economy. With the right mix of sustained investment, public-private collaboration and strong regional integration, its digital awakening holds great promise for inclusive and sustainable economic growth.

B. The e-commerce leap in Kenya: advancing inclusion in a fast-evolving digital economy

Kenya has emerged as a leading digital economy in Africa, powered by extensive mobile networks, fintech innovation and strong private sector engagement. Its experience illustrates how inclusive digital transformation, backed by strategic planning, can unlock new opportunities for economic participation, particularly for MSMEs, women and marginalized groups.

1. Strong digital infrastructure, financial inclusion and private sector innovation powering e-commerce growth

Kenya ranks third in Africa's e-commerce market, with a value of $0.9 billion in 2024.[4] That growth is underpinned by a robust digital infrastructure, including more than 22.7 million Internet users (approximately 41 per cent of the population) and 66 million active mobile connections, representing a 119 per cent penetration rate.[5] A key enabler of that trend is financial inclusion, with more than 84.8 per cent of adults having access to formal financial services through bank or mobile money accounts, thanks largely to the M-Pesa mobile wallet.[6]

The vibrant private sector has played a pivotal role in translating that digital and financial access into a dynamic e-commerce ecosystem. Telecommunication firms, fintech start-ups, retailers and banks are leading innovation in mobile payments, online ordering, QR payments and buy-now-pay-later models. Safaricom, the country's largest mobile operator, anchors the market with its M-Pesa mobile money network and the Masoko e-commerce marketplace.

MSMEs, which contribute about 35 per cent of gross domestic product and employ more than 80 per cent of the workforce, are increasingly moving online, often starting with social media storefronts before transitioning to formal e-commerce platforms. Support programmes, from technology hubs to financial start-ups, are propelling that shift by offering merchant loans, digital tools and marketing solutions. Notably, more than half of adults made daily mobile money transactions in 2024, up from 24 per cent in 2021, underscoring the central role of e-payments in everyday commerce. Such private initiatives align with public efforts to expand digital access nationwide.

2. People-centred e-commerce strategy

The National E-commerce Strategy, launched in December 2023,[7] marks a major milestone in the country's digital transformation journey. To implement the Strategy effectively, Kenya has established robust governance mechanisms, including an interministerial e-commerce committee and a dedicated coordination unit. The Strategy is supported by broader national initiatives, such as the National Digital Master Plan (2022–2032) and Vision 2030, which continue to expand information and communications technology (ICT) infrastructure and broadband connectivity. Complementary legal reforms, including new consumer protection regulations under development, aim to create an enabling regulatory environment for secure and inclusive e-commerce growth.

With a bold vision, to make online commerce accessible to all, the Strategy puts people at the centre of the digital economy, ensuring that no one, including marginalized and underserved groups, is left behind. Jointly developed by the Ministry of Information, Communications and

---

4 See https://www.statista.com.

5 See https://datareportal.com/reports/digital-2024-kenya.

6 See centralbank.go.ke/wp-content/uploads/2024/12/2024-FINACCESS-HOUSEHOLD-SURVEY-MAIN-REPORT.pdf.

7 See https://www.ca.go.ke/sites/default/files/CA/E-Commerce%20Strategy/National%20E-Commerce%20Strategy%20%202023.pdf.

the Digital Economy and the Ministry of Trade, Investments and Industry, with support from GIZ and UNCTAD, the Strategy is aimed at building a trusted and inclusive e-commerce ecosystem that promotes equitable participation across all regions and demographics.

Inclusivity is a central pillar of the Strategy. Building on insights from the UNCTAD-supported eT Ready[8] and extensive consultations with organizations advocating for the rights and inclusion of persons with disabilities, the Strategy incorporates targeted measures to ensure accessibility in digital platforms. That aligns with broader national efforts, such as the Kenya Bureau of Standards, which introduced accessibility standards for ICT products and services in 2022, requiring that both public and private digital services be accessible to persons with disabilities, in collaboration with inABLE, a non-profit organization that empowers the blind and visually impaired.

Goal 5 of the Strategy on skills and human capacity champions the design of accessibility e-commerce platforms and calls for incentive packages to support e-commerce ventures led by persons with disabilities, alongside those led by women and youth. By addressing structural barriers, the Strategy seeks to empower rural populations, persons with disabilities and other excluded groups to actively engage in and benefit from the digital economy.

The push for inclusivity extends beyond the borders of Kenya through strategic alignment with regional and continental frameworks. The Strategy complements the EAC E-commerce Strategy and the Digital Trade Protocol of the African Continental Free Trade Area, helping to harmonize standards on consumer protection, data flows and digital payments. Those efforts are aimed at opening new markets and ensuring that Kenyan e-sellers – including women, youth and persons with disabilities – can engage more equitably in cross-border digital trade.

3. Women in the digital economy

Kenya has made meaningful strides in empowering women's participation in the digital economy. High Internet and mobile penetration have enabled many women to bypass traditional market barriers, with social media and mobile-based platforms providing flexible, accessible opportunities, especially for those balancing business with caregiving responsibilities. A streamlined business registration process, requiring only 23 days, has further reduced bureaucratic hurdles that tend to disproportionately affect women due to time constraints, lower access to intermediaries and limited legal familiarity.

Mobile money, digital payments and microfinance platforms have provided new pathways for women without access to formal banking services to engage in trade, However, critical gender-specific challenges remain. Access to finance continues to be a major barrier as women entrepreneurs are less likely to have collateral or formal credit histories and often face higher interest rates or loan rejection, despite the country's strong credit information systems.

Tax compliance and digital literacy gaps also pose challenges for women-led businesses, especially in rural areas, where navigating complex tax obligations or unfamiliar e-commerce tools can be disproportionately difficult without adequate support. Nevertheless, a strong culture of innovation and peer collaboration is helping to bridge those gaps with women-led networks promoting digital skills, mentorship and market access.

The experience of Kenya highlights that enabling infrastructure and supportive business environments can significantly lower barriers for women. Achieving true gender equity in the digital economy requires sustained policy attention on financing, skills development and the unique constraints women face.

8 See https://unctad.org/system/files/official-document/dtlecdc2022d2_en.pdf.

4. Next steps for inclusive growth

The digital transformation of Kenya is gaining strong momentum, anchored by its inclusive National E-commerce Strategy. While some challenges remain, such as expanding digital access to women, youth and rural populations, reducing transaction and logistics costs for small businesses and strengthening legal frameworks for consumer protection, these obstacles present clear opportunities for continued growth and innovation. The commitment of Kenya to closing those gaps through targeted policies, capacity-building and improved infrastructure is creating an enabling environment in which all citizens can benefit from digital commerce.

Collaborative efforts among government, private sector and development partners, such as UNCTAD, GIZ, the European Union and the World Bank, are driving this process forward. As Cabinet Secretary Eliud Owalo aptly stated: "This e-commerce strategy is a big leap towards addressing the bottlenecks that have been stifling e-commerce in the country for many years." With sustained dedication to inclusivity and innovation, Kenya is poised to unlock the full potential of its digital economy, fostering sustainable, equitable growth that reaches every corner of society.

C. Digital momentum in Vanuatu: a model of e-commerce leadership in the Pacific

Vanuatu is emerging as a compelling example among Pacific small island developing States of how inclusive digital transformation can be achieved through strong institutions, local innovation and effective regional partnerships. While facing constraints in relation to isolation and infrastructure, the country has strategically invested in building a vibrant and inclusive digital economy. The experience of Vanuatu offers a replicable model for other small island developing States charting their own digital futures.

1. Institutional leadership for inclusive e-commerce

Vanuatu stands out among small island developing States for its dedicated institutional architecture to support e-commerce development. Central to its progress is the establishment of a dedicated E-commerce Unit within the Ministry of Tourism, Trade, Commerce and of Ni-Vanuatu Businesses, and business activities and economic development initiatives that are focused specifically on its native population, the Ni-Vanuatu people. Both of which play a key role in coordinating national and regional digital trade efforts. The Unit leads the implementation of the National E-commerce Strategy and Roadmap, developed in 2022 with support from development partners, which is aimed at accelerating e-commerce adoption, increasing digital readiness, supporting economic transformation and unlocking the potential of digital trade across the archipelago.[9] The Strategy adopts a comprehensive approach to digital trade and provides a clear road map for strengthening the digital economy and integrating Vanuatu into regional and global value chains.

A cornerstone of the country's approach is the National E-commerce Committee, a multi-stakeholder body guiding implementation across the strategic priority areas, including infrastructure, legal frameworks, trade logistics, payments, digital skills, financing and SME support. The Committee brings together representatives from the Government, the private sector, academia and civil society, ensuring inclusive and coordinated action. Together, those institutional mechanisms provide a high level of policy coherence and stakeholder engagement, offering a model for how small economies can institutionalize digital transformation efforts to drive inclusive growth.

2. Local innovation and ecosystem strengthening

The digital transition initiatives of Vanuatu, spearheaded by the Government, are reinforced by local innovation and community-driven initiatives. The Vanuatu Innovation and Digital Economy Association (V-IDEA) plays a pivotal role in convening digital entrepreneurs, advocating for enabling policies and nurturing collaboration within the technology ecosystem.[10] Meanwhile, the V-Lab e-commerce incubator supports early-stage start-ups and MSMEs through technical training, mentorship and access to digital tools. Its mission is to empower local entrepreneurs, especially youth and women, to build resilient, future-ready businesses. The Association has delivered more than 300 free technical workshops and training sessions on topics such as e-commerce, coding, virtual reality, three-dimensional printing, the Internet of things and digital payments. Since its inception, it has assisted more than 150 entrepreneurs through mixed-duration programmes (ranging from one week to a full year) and has provided leadership and

9 The Strategy was prepared as part of the project on "Strengthening an inclusive enabling environment for e-commerce in Tonga and Vanuatu", which was implemented by TradeWorthy and funded by the Department of Foreign Affairs and Trade of Australia. Financial support for the launch of the Strategy was also provided by EIF and the European Union.

10 Established in 20210, V-IDEA acts as a bridge between government and grass-roots innovators, amplifying local voices in national and regional dialogue. See https://vanuatu-idea.com.

digital skills training to more than 300 young people as part of its Yut Pawa programme between 2023 and 2024. It also implemented the first digital incubator in 2024, funded by the Pacific Agreement on Closer Economic Relations (PACER) Plus and supported by the Government, the Chamber of Commerce and V-Lab. Working in close partnership with development actors, V-Lab delivers targeted support in areas such as digital marketing, online sales and financial literacy. Supported entrepreneurs have great potential and the success of their projects is having a significant impact on the business and digital ecosystem.

To sustain the momentum and foster knowledge exchange, Vanuatu hosts an annual E-commerce Symposium, which has been running since 2021. The event brings together stakeholders across sectors to share best practices, celebrate local success stories and align priorities for digital development. It serves as a key platform for advancing dialogue and maintaining visibility. In May 2025, the initiative evolved into a broader Digital Week on the theme "Innovate today, sustain tomorrow". The four-day event, held in Santo, integrated the E-commerce Symposium, Consumer Rights Day and National ICT Days to create a unified platform for raising awareness, showcasing innovation and mobilizing cross-sector collaboration in support of a resilient and inclusive digital economy.[11]

3. Regional cooperation as a catalyst of digital growth

The digital progress of Vanuatu is closely tied to regional cooperation and multilateral support, with the Pacific E-commerce Initiative, led by the PIF secretariat, playing a central role.[12] Through that Initiative, Vanuatu has benefited from capacity-building, technical assistance and strategic alignment with the Pacific Regional E-commerce Strategy and Roadmap (2021–2025). Through that initiative, Vanuatu has benefited from regionally tailored capacity-building, technical assistance and peer learning opportunities that have accelerated its digital progress. The country's institutional and technical advancements have also been reinforced by development partners working in close collaboration.

Among them, UNCTAD has been instrumental in that process, with its eT Ready in 2018, in which it identified key policy gaps and set the stage for strategic interventions. That led to the development of the Vanuatu National E-commerce Strategy and Roadmap (2022), which UNCTAD supported alongside capacity-building workshops, stakeholder coordination and implementation monitoring, including through its broader eTrade for all initiative. Complementing those efforts, the United Nations Capital Development Fund, through the Pacific Digital Economy Programme, a joint initiative with UNDP and UNCTAD, has focused on advancing digital finance and expanding access to digital services, particularly in remote and underserved communities, along with region-wide research and capacity-building activities. EIF has also contributed to strengthening trade-related institutional capacities, while the European Union has supported investments in ICT infrastructure and legal reform. The World Bank has supported major infrastructure projects in the ICT sector and payments-related areas. Collectively, those partnerships have contributed to laying a strong foundation for digital inclusion in Vanuatu, with targeted programmes that empower MSMEs, women and youth, ensuring that the benefits of digital trade are widely shared across society.

[11] See https://digitalweek.gov.vu/index.php.

[12] The Initiative fosters peer learning and policy harmonization among Pacific nations, enabling countries such as Vanuatu to scale up their digital economy efforts, while advancing common standards and regulatory coherence across the region.

4. Addressing constraints to accelerate progress

Despite strong momentum in digital development, several challenges continue to be important barriers to e-commerce growth. Chief among those are Internet connectivity and affordability, further constrained by limited access to electricity, especially in rural areas. While digital literacy has improved, driven by local initiatives and training programmes, it still requires deeper investment, especially among older populations and small business owners unfamiliar with digital platforms. Payment interoperability and logistics continue to impede MSMEs from fully participating in regional and global marketplaces due to limited payment gateway options and unreliable delivery systems. Those challenges are compounded by broader structural constraints such as high shipping costs, limited economies of scale and vulnerability to climate-related disruptions.

Nevertheless, the experience of Vanuatu offers valuable lessons for other small island developing States navigating similar challenges. Its approach, anchored in strong institutional leadership, inclusive multi-stakeholder collaboration and grass-roots innovation, demonstrates how tailored strategies can effectively bridge the digital divide. Initiatives such as V-Lab and V-IDEA exemplify how community-driven innovation can complement national policy efforts, ensuring that digital growth is inclusive and resilient. While gaps in infrastructure, skills and logistics remain, the country's commitment to inclusion, policy coherence and regional alignment has created a solid foundation for sustainable digital transformation. Its experience underscores that context-specific e-commerce strategies, integrated within broader digital transformation efforts, can contribute to bridge the digital divide and generate broad-based opportunities for economic transformation.

Annex II

Methodology

Implementation reviews apply a monitoring methodology to assess progress and gaps and document good practices, policy impacts and lessons learned in the implementation of the recommendations, actions and measures derived from a national or regional reference document, such as an assessment (eTrade Readiness Assessment (eT Ready) or eT Ready-based), or a key reference policy document (e.g. action plan, e-commerce strategy or policy).[1] Only countries with a reference document finalized by June 2024 have been considered in the review.

Table
Overview of the participation of eTrade partner countries in various implementation reviews

	Document (published/ delivered)	Implementation review				Country reviewed at least once
		First	Second	Third	Fourth	
Africa						
Benin	eTR (2020), ECS (2021)					
Botswana	ECS (2021)					
Burkina Faso	eTR (2018)	✓	✓	✓	✓	✓
Côte d'Ivoire	eTR (2021), ECS (2024)		✓	✓	✓	✓
Ghana	eTR (2023), ECS (2024)					
Kenya	eTR (2022), ECS (2023)			✓	✓	✓
Lesotho	eTR (2019)	✓				✓
Liberia	eTR (2018)					
Madagascar	eTR (2018)	✓	✓	✓		✓

[1] An action plan is aimed at assisting countries in prioritizing the implementation of recommendations resulting from an eT Ready, formulating projects to be carried out within a 12-month time frame, securing partnerships and financial support from various partners. They are designed to be flexible and adaptable, enabling rapid adjustments to evolving circumstances and priorities. An e-commerce strategy is a document meant to be formally endorsed by a Government (in the case of a country). It generally includes a vision and mission statement, strategic goals and initiatives outlined in an implementation plan, covering several priority policy areas that support e-commerce development. Strategies typically span a period of up to five years; include governance and monitoring and evaluation frameworks; and devise a whole-of-government response, which is integrated into the public agenda in line with national development objectives and aimed at promoting an enabling e-commerce environment in the short to medium term. An e-commerce strategy can be framed within a national e-commerce policy, a strategic framework established by a Government to regulate and promote e-commerce or vice versa, depending on specific country requirements.

	Document (published/ delivered)	Implementation review				Country reviewed at least once
		First	Second	Third	Fourth	
Malawi	eTR (2020), eTR-AP (2025)		✓	✓	✓	✓
Mali	eTR (2020)			✓		✓
Mauritania	eTR (2024), ECS (ongoing)				✓	✓
Niger	eTR (2020), ECS (ongoing)		✓	✓	✓	✓
Rwanda	ECS (2023), ECP				✓	✓
Senegal	eTR (2018), ECS (2019)	✓	✓	✓	✓	✓
Togo	eTR (2018), ECS (2021)	✓	✓	✓	✓	✓
Tunisia	eTR (2022), eTR-AP (2022)			✓	✓	✓
Uganda	eTR (2018)	✓	✓	✓	✓	✓
United Republic of Tanzania	eTR (2020), ECS (2025)				✓	✓
Zambia	eTR (2018)	✓	✓	✓	✓	✓
Asia						
Afghanistan	eTR (2019)					
Bangladesh	eTR (2019), ECP (2020)			✓	✓	✓
Bhutan	eTR (2017), ECP (2021)	✓	✓			✓
Cambodia	eTR (2017), ECS (2020)	✓	✓		✓	✓
Iraq	eTR (2020)			✓		✓
Jordan	eTR (2022), ECS (2023)				✓	✓
Lao People's Democratic Republic	eTR (2018)					
Mongolia	eTR (2023)				✓	✓
Myanmar	eTR (2018), ECS (2021)	✓				✓
Nepal	eTR (2017), ECS (2019)	✓	✓	✓	✓	✓
Pacific						
Cook Islands	Other (2023)					

	Document (published/ delivered)	Implementation review				Country reviewed at least once
		First	Second	Third	Fourth	
Fiji	eComAss (2020), ECS (2025)					
Kiribati	eTR (2019), ECS (ongoing)					
Micronesia (Federated States of)	eComAss (2020)					
Nauru	eComAss (2021)					
Niue	eComAss (2020)					
Papua New Guinea	eComAss (2020), ECS (2024)			✓		✓
Samoa	eTR (2017), ECS (2022), ECP (ongoing)	✓		✓	✓	✓
Solomon Islands	eTR (2018), ECS (2023)		✓	✓	✓	✓
Tonga	eComAss (2020), ECS (2021)			✓	✓	✓
Tuvalu	eTR (2019), ECS (2023)		✓	✓	✓	✓
Vanuatu	eTR (2018), ECS (2022)	✓			✓	✓
Others						
Peru	eTR (2023)				✓	✓
TOTAL	**43**	**13**	**14**	**20**	**23**	**31**

Abbreviations: e-commerce assessment (eComAss), eT Ready (eTR), eT Ready action plan (eTR-AP), e-commerce strategy/policy (ECS/ECP), other type of strategic document (other). In blue: done with support from the United Nations Conference on Trade and Development (UNCTAD). In green: based on UNCTAD methodology.

Implementation reviews are a central component of the eTrade Implementation Support Mechanism, which relies on a network of national eTrade focal points, mainly senior government officials in trade ministries or other entities with a recognized leadership role in the area of e-commerce. They have regularly engaged in activities related to the Implementation Support Mechanism and benefited from capacity-building workshops. The focal points are instrumental in ensuring multi-stakeholder engagement for the implementation reviews, for example by identifying, sensitizing and mobilizing key public and private sector resource persons.

Methodological improvements, contextual adaptations and lessons learned from earlier reviews have allowed UNCTAD to better capture the diverse realities and reform progress across participating countries. The updated methodology is structured around four main phases, which took place between November 2024 and September 2025. Those phases have been dedicated to: (a) updating the review methodology and customizing and testing the questionnaire; (b) engaging with stakeholders to build capacities; (c) collecting, verifying and analysing the data and drafting the report; and (d) reviewing and obtaining feedback from stakeholders and finalizing, editing and publishing the report.

Figure
Four main phases of the updated methodology

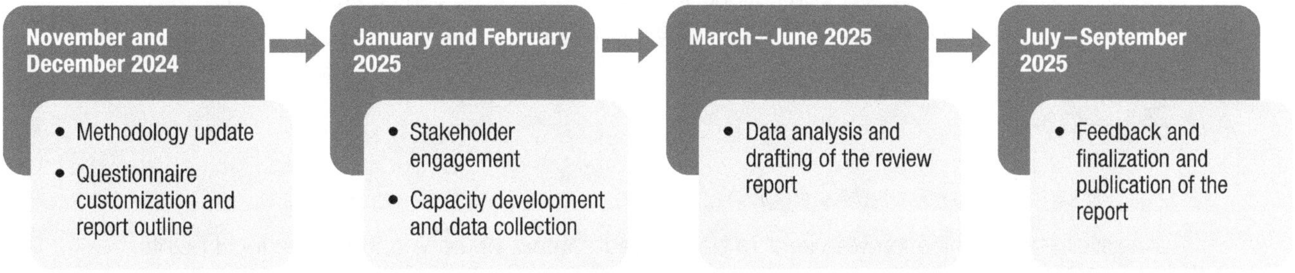

A. Phase 1

1. Methodology update

The revised methodology reflects both the diversity of partner countries and the varying stages of reform implementation. Unlike previous reviews, which focused primarily on countries assessed between 2017 and 2020, mainly least developed countries, the scope of the present review has been expanded. It includes countries that developed various e-commerce reference documents, such as e-commerce assessments based on UNCTAD methodology conducted by other development partners, or an eT Ready action plan, e-commerce strategy or policy supported by UNCTAD.

As a result, the present review departs from the typical eT Ready structure based on seven policy areas and is shaped along two main pillars. The first pillar is focused on the quality of the e-commerce policymaking processes and implementation of reforms enabling e-commerce. The second pillar highlights, in selected areas, developments within the broader digital and e-commerce ecosystem. That shift allows a more holistic and flexible assessment of e-commerce enabling reform efforts carried out by the reviewed countries, regardless of the specific reference document used, as some countries have a combination of them. In accordance with the approach piloted in previous reviews, the scored performance assessment model has been phased out, in favour of a more impact-centred, narrative-driven analysis. That approach captures qualitative insights to reform implementation, including persistent challenges and emerging opportunities. To illustrate those dynamics in a practical and country-specific format, case studies for Cambodia, Kenya and Vanuatu are presented in annex I, reflecting diverse regional and developmental contexts. The case studies offer grounded insights into country-led reform processes, illustrating what has worked, what remains challenging and where future support could be most effectively targeted.

2. Questionnaire customization and report outline

The questionnaire remains central to the review process. Continuously refined across iterations, it has been updated to better reflect the realities and evolving needs of participating countries. Its primary goals are to document the impact, lessons learned and challenges in implementing reforms related to e-commerce and to highlight good practices and successful initiatives. To improve data quality and engagement, the questionnaire contains “good reporting tips” that encourage responding countries to: (a) actively involve stakeholders, including line ministries, regulatory agencies and civil society; (b) strategically plan data collection and identify early on the required inputs and responsible entities; (c) provide evidence-based data to highlight progress and impacts, referencing sources explicitly; (d) focus on new developments, especially relevant for a country that has participated in previous reviews; and (e) enhance the visibility of successful initiatives by including quotes, pictures and specific examples. In parallel, UNCTAD prepared an annotated report outline to support national focal points in aligning contributions with the revised methodology and to ensure consistency in the final reporting structure.

B. Phase 2

1. Stakeholder engagement

An official communication was sent to designated contact persons and eTrade focal points, primarily those in trade-related ministries in partner countries of the Implementation Support Mechanism, to anchor the review process within national administrations. That step formally recognized the role of the focal points in each country and ensured their engagement. The respective Permanent Missions in Geneva were also involved; their support was instrumental in fostering the commitment of their respective capitals and, in some cases, identifying new focal points.

2. Capacity development and data collection

To support a shared understanding of the review process and its objectives, an online capacity-building workshop was held on 28 and 29 January 2025. The workshop was divided into three sessions covering French-speaking countries in Africa, English-speaking countries in Africa and Asia, and countries in Latin America and the Caribbean and the Pacific. Participants included focal points and other relevant national stakeholders, such as line ministries, regulators and other public sector agencies, as well as private sector representatives whose capacities to engage in the review process were meaningfully strengthened.[2]

Following the workshop, the data collection questionnaire was shared with all partner countries. Throughout February 2025, UNCTAD regularly followed up to maximize timely responses, with deadlines extensions granted on a case-by-case basis. Data collection was complemented by interviews and exchanges with senior officials from regional organizations.

C. Phase 3

UNCTAD carried out a comprehensive analysis and quality review of all questionnaire responses, complemented by additional desk research. The analytical process enabled the synthesis of a significant volume of country-specific data and insights. The drafting of the report took place between March and June 2025, reflecting both the breadth and depth of the material collected.

2 A total of 248 persons registered for the three sessions and benefited from shared resources (video recording and presentation), while 126 participants, including 53 women and 73 men, attended the live segments with question-and-answer sessions. Representatives from 20 countries participated, namely: 12 countries from Africa; 4 countries from Asia; 3 countries from the Pacific; and 1 country from Latin America and the Caribbean. Most of the participants came from the public sector. Participants expressed appreciation for the engagement of stakeholders and the implementation review process of UNCTAD, recognizing its role in coordinating efforts, gathering critical data and accelerating the implementation of eT Ready and e-commerce strategy priority measures. They recognized how those implementation reviews helped to identify initiatives needing additional support and signalled gaps in implementation. They also stressed their role in strengthening the linkages between the lead ministry and the private sector to ensure effective policy cohesion and execution. Some clarifications were requested on the methodology and timeline of the review, which were promptly addressed. More than 90 per cent of the respondents rated the quality of the presentations as either "good" or "excellent" and found the discussions were either "satisfactorily" or "significantly" open and inclusive. Some 91 per cent of the respondents agreed that the format of the event had been adequate in terms of timing, length and structure.

D. Phase 4

By the end of June 2025, the draft of the report was circulated internally and to external parties, including eTrade focal points and eTrade for all partners. The feedback was instrumental in enhancing the report's evidence base and ensuring factual accuracy. Editing, layout, translation into French and printing were completed by September 2025 for public release and dissemination in the context of the sixteenth session of United Nations Conference on Trade and Development (20–23 October 2025, Geneva).

Throughout the report, cross-cutting themes, such as gender mainstreaming, youth engagement, rural community support and persons with disabilities, are integrated where relevant. Emphasis is also given to addressing the persistent lack of reliable statistics related to e-commerce, recognizing that inclusive and sustainable digital development depends on data-driven policymaking. While the primary focus of the report is on e-commerce, the broader context of digital trade (defined as all trade that is digitally ordered and/or delivered) must be kept in mind.[3] Many of the bottlenecks identified, such as infrastructure gaps, regulatory barriers and skills shortages, apply to both e-commerce and digital trade. The solutions proposed within that framework, therefore, are intended to facilitate not only e-commerce development but also digital trade more broadly.

[3] E-commerce refers specifically to the sale or purchase of goods and services conducted over computer networks by methods designed for placing and receiving orders (i.e. "digitally ordered"). Digital trade encompasses all international trade that is either digitally ordered (international e-commerce) or digitally delivered. Therefore, digital trade includes not only international e-commerce transactions but also services delivered remotely through digital means. At the same time, digital trade excludes domestic e-commerce transactions between buyers and sellers resident in the same economic territory. For further precisions on e-commerce and digital trade, see UNCTAD (2023a).